From Washington—
"Until I read *WINNING THROUGH INTIMIDATION*, I only had a vague intuitive idea of what was really happening. Anyone involved in negotiating anything should read Mr. Ringer's book first."

—PAUL H. PFLEGER

From Arizona—
"I couldn't put it down. It is one of the best books of its kind that I have ever come across."

—DR. CHARLES W. SKOUSON

From Oregon—
"I only wish I'd had your book or known you long years ago."

—THOMAS G. STALEY

From Colorado—
"I have just finished reading your book, *WINNING THROUGH INTIMIDATION*, and found it to be the most absorbing and accurate in the "how to" field that I have ever read."

—J. R. BETTS

From Delaware—
"I appreciate having had the privilege to have read your book (2 times). It put many thoughts of mine into words."

—GEORGE H. H. GARRISON

Winning Through Intimidation

BY

Robert J. Ringer

Illustrations by Jack Medoff

FAWCETT CREST • NEW YORK

WINNING THROUGH INTIMIDATION

THIS BOOK CONTAINS THE COMPLETE TEXT OF THE
ORIGINAL HARDCOVER EDITION.

Published by Fawcett Books, CBS Publications,
CBS Consumer Publishing, a Division of CBS Inc.,
by arrangement with Los Angeles Book Publishers Co.

Copyright © 1973 by Robert J. Ringer

Copyright © 1974 by Robert J. Ringer

ISBN: 0-449-23589-0

Alternate Selection of the Literary Guild

Printed in the United States of America

21   20   19

Dedicated to the promoters of the world —from the chairman of the board of the largest corporation to the initiator of the smallest one-man project—to whom civilization owes its very existence, and upon whose shoulders rests the future of mankind.

Contents

SECTION III
THE TECHNIQUES I USED TO WIN

Translation: *How I Applied My Philosophy To My Specific Objective*

SECTION IV
LEAPFROGGING TORTOISE HITS THE JACKPOT

Translation: *My Understanding Of Intimidation Pays Off*

Introduction

Try as I did, I was not able to come up with a more appropriate opening punch for this book than the one used by Ayn Rand—a philosopher-writer eons ahead of her time—in her masterpiece, *The Virtue of Selfishness*.

In that ingenious work, she opens by saying: "The title of this book may evoke the kind of question that I hear once in a while: 'Why do you use the word "selfishness" to denote virtuous qualities of character, when that word antagonizes so many people to whom it does not mean the things you mean?'

"To those who ask it, my answer is: 'For the reason that makes you afraid of it.' "

Likewise, when I tagged my book with the label of *Winning Through Intimidation*, I knew that it would evoke a conditioned-response reaction from many, that the goody-two-shoes disciples of unreality would be offended, and that it would cause some people to wonder: "Why do you use the word 'intimidation' when you know that word will antagonize so many people to whom it does not mean the things you mean?"

A la Ayn Rand—To those who ask it, my answer is: "For the reason that makes you afraid of it."

So many, many books begin with an approach such as: "There have been a great number of books written on this subject, many of them very helpful, but none have organized the principles into easy-to-understand form. I therefore saw the need to fill this great void, and thus . . . etc., etc., etc." Sound familiar?

Well, I'm going to set the tone of *Winning Through Intimidation* early by telling you that even though there have been a multitude of books written on the subject of "success" (in business, love, and life in general), I *don't* think that many of them have been very helpful. In fact, I have long contended that most of them (including some of the more famous best-sellers) have been very *harmful* to millions of people who have blindly followed their rhetoric without making the principles expounded upon stand up to the realities of life.

Such books specifically avoid these realities, lacking the daring to tell it like it really is rather than the way people would like "it" to be.

Having read book after book and thus becoming firmly convinced, after stripping away all of the flowery words, that they were little more than carbon copies of one another, it occurred to me that the average reader—the guy who goes out into the world every day and gets his head bashed in by the hard realities—might be fed up with the fantasy that most "success" books preach.

With that I give you *Winning Through Intimidation,* a book that deals in reality rather than wishes. Ahead of its time? I really can't say. I can only look around me every day and conclude that most people, at present, are *not* facing reality.

Perhaps *Winning Through Intimidation* is not ahead of its time at all. Perhaps there will never be a time for reality on this planet. Maybe reality was only meant to be practiced elsewhere in our universe.

I'll close the chit-chat portion of this book by pointing out (for reasons that will later become apparent) that I've been aware, from the beginning, that there are three types of people who will not relate to the contents of *Winning Through Intimidation:*

1) The "Mister McGoos," who will blast through each chapter without having a deep thought and, when finished, be firmly convinced that they have just read a book on how to sell real estate. They will have missed the whole point—but then, Mister McGoos always do. To them the book will forever be a publication on the principles of selling real estate, and nothing I could ever say would convince them otherwise.

They simply will not be able to comprehend that *Winning Through Intimidation* is a book on the philosophy of reality, that its basic principles apply not only to every other type of business, but to life in general, and that the specific *techniques* (regarding real estate) described in the book serve only as *examples* of how to apply its truisms to a specific business or specific aspect of life.

2) The "Ostriches," who as always will hide their heads in the sands of fantasy and chastise The Tortoise for concocting such an "ugly" philosophy. As Ostriches, they go through life labeling all that is new, different or enlightening as "evil," and all that is old, constant or suppressing as "good." As unrealists, they cannot understand that the truth—no matter how painful—is always, by its very nature, "good," and that any lie—regardless of how pleasant—is always, by its very nature, "bad."

3) The "Tell-It-Like-It-Is" folks, those honest, straightforward souls who will simply think that I'm a lousy writer. God bless the Straightforward; without them I don't know where we'd all be.

Naturally I hope that *Winning Through Intimidation* rates high on your list. But if not, then for your sake I hope that you at least fall into the third category above. I don't wish upon anyone a life of being a Mister McGoo or an Ostrich.

—The Tortoise

SECTION I

DEMOLITION
AND
CONSTRUCTION

*Translation: Laying The
Groundwork for Winning.*

Chapter 1

Shattering The Myths

Translation: *What DOESN'T work.*

In order to construct a new, efficient, "workable" building on a site where an old, inefficient, "unworkable" building exists, you first have to raze the older structure. And that's exactly how I'm going to begin this book, by tearing down the old—by shattering a couple of myths that have been used to brainwash people for generations. It will be much easier for me to describe how I constructed a workable philosophy if I first explain to you what I have found, through actual experience, doesn't work.

After cutting away the fat, the overriding message in many "success" and "how to" books is: If a person has a "positive mental attitude" and works "hard, long hours," he will ultimately succeed. The approaches of the authors often border on mysticism rather than reality and logic.

I've known many, many frustrated salesmen and businessmen who have become very charged up after reading some well known "success" books, only to go out, week after week, month after month, year after year, and fail to achieve their goals, notwithstanding the fact that they practiced the principles of these books religiously. The illusions created by the oftentimes flowery and enthusiastic wording are exciting, but the reality that confronts a man when he goes out into the business-world jungle and gets clawed and kicked is quite another thing. Such a man becomes confused and frustrated because no one in the jungle seems to care that he has a positive attitude or that he works hard. His only hope is to cling to the word "ultimately;" the books say that "ultimately" success will come.

Like millions of other people, I fell into the trap of believing that my great reward would ultimately come if I just worked hard and continued to display a positive mental attitude. But the reward *didn't* come, not until I analyzed my own frustrating and brutal experiences and figured out, logically, why the myths I had blindly accepted did not work; then proved to myself, through more firsthand experience, what did work.

What kept me sidetracked for so many years, and I believe has kept millions of others hooked on illusory myths, was that I couldn't understand why so many of these basic "success" rules did not work for me if they worked for their apparently successful authors.

I used to discuss these "success" books with a friend of mine who was the head of an insurance agency. He intrigued me because, on the surface, he was the most unlikely candidate for success, particularly in the field of selling, whom I'd ever observed; yet he had done extremely well in his field. He not only gave very little outward indication of a positive mental attitude, but he probably worked fewer hours than anyone I knew. He was also very quiet, shy and awkward. Respecting his opinion because of the results I had seen him obtain, I asked him why the methods of many supposedly successful authors of "success" books did not seem to work in actual practice. His answer astonished me:

He said that successful men rarely know the real reasons for their success, even though they always think they know. He added that this is caused by the fact that they're too close to the forest to see the trees. That explanation had a big effect on me; if I couldn't rely on the traditional advice of successful people, what could I rely on? It finally became apparent that the only solution was to develop my own philosophy and techniques, based on my own personal experience.

As I pointed out, the reason my friend's opinions had credibility with me was because I had been able to observe the results he himself had obtained, even though he didn't do the things that "successful" salesmen were "supposed" to do. His own success, of and by itself, was myth shattering in that it destroyed the mental picture I had in my mind of the typical "good salesman."

As a general rule, I found that men whom others constantly characterize as "great salesmen" usually are not even good salesmen. The fact that they're labeled "great salesmen" is oftentimes the very reason they really aren't. Because of their reputations as "great salesmen," they pose a visible threat just by entering a room. Eventually it became easy for me to spot these unsuccessful "successful salesmen," and I adopted a pet phrase to describe them: *All show and no dough.*

If most successful men couldn't see the trees because they were too close to the forest, then how did they dream up all of those unworkable "success" rules—rules that I had read about in so many books? My conclusions were as follows:

1) Because of the brainwashing of society, successful men, like everyone else, naturally absorb the "success" myths handed down over the years, even though they may not actually practice them. As a result, a "conditioned-response" pattern develops whereby they automatically regurgitate phrases about "positive mental attitude" and "working hard, long hours" when asked how they attained their lofty stations in life.

2) Society—that same menacing abstract entity —also manages to make most successful people feel guilty about their success, at least subconsciously. As a result, they're almost afraid to outwardly acknowledge the realities of how they really made their money.

3) Finally, I suspect that there are cases where authors of "how to" books have, for commercial reasons, purposely withheld the realities of their success. Some of the more popularly known "success" rules are much easier to sell than reality.

Once I understood why the rules laid down in many "success" and "how to" books weren't necessarily valid, my mind was free to analyze the very cornerstones of "success" mythology—namely, "positive mental attitude" and "working hard, long hours."

As to positive mental attitude, I found that most men have a completely distorted concept of what it even is. They think of it as a cause of success, when in fact it's more a result of being prepared. You don't acquire a positive mental attitude by standing in front of a mirror like a robot and repeating positive slogans to yourself over and over again; nor do you obtain it by repetition of thought; and certainly you don't achieve a positive mental attitude just by heartily shaking a person's hand, smiling from ear to ear, and loudly exclaiming, "Great!", when asked how things are going.

Through my own experience, I learned that striving for a positive mental attitude will get you nowhere unless you have the ammunition to back it up. You develop a positive mental attitude by being prepared, by understanding the realities of what it takes to succeed, and by being good at the necessary techniques. It's a cycle: the more prepared a person is, the more positive his attitude, and, therefore, the better his chances of succeeding. It's wonderful for a person to have a goal to close a million dollar deal within, say, six months, but if he's not prepared—if he is not ready for the accomplishment—then regardless of what he tries to tell himself, he won't really believe—in his subconscious mind—that he can do it.

What I did was carefully and honestly study my own experiences, analyzing what had contributed to my failures and what had contributed to my successes, then pieced together an overall philosophy based on those things that had generated the positive results. Although there have been no basic changes in my philosophy for a long time, refinement of the details never ceases; each new experience teaches me a different little twist.

But even though I shattered the hoaxes about acquiring a positive mental attitude and discovered that it could be developed only by being prepared, there was still a problem. I would venture out into the jungle, sincerely believing that I could make sales because I was prepared, only to end up having my teeth kicked in by the hard realities—realities that my preparedness had no control over. I'd fail in my attempt to make a sale, then fail in a second attempt, a third and a fourth; it was only a matter of time—perhaps after the tenth, the fifteenth or twentieth straight unsuccessful sales attempt—until my ego and self-image were shattered, and, finally, my belief along with them. The result was confusion and doubt. I would go back and restudy my experiences and observations, only to find, once again, that my original analysis had been sound after all.

It finally occurred to me that what I had been lacking was a method for *sustaining* a positive mental attitude in the face of a series of consecutive failures. Because I believed in my basic analysis and because I knew I was prepared, I was able to rationally arrive at a conclusion that evolved into one of my earliest theories. This theory caused a major shift upward in my career, and I could never have earned, and received, substantial income without it as an integral part of my philosophy. It's called the

THEORY OF SUSTENANCE OF A POSITIVE ATTITUDE THROUGH THE ASSUMPTION OF A NEGATIVE RESULT

Whenever I relate this theory to anyone, the idea of maintaining a positive mental attitude by assuming failure always seems to unbalance them. Nevertheless it makes sense; it's simply a matter of reality.

This theory doesn't mean that a person should enter a sales situation (almost any situation in life can be classified as a "sales situation") feeling that he *can't* make the sale. What he should do is realistically assume that he *won't* make the sale. The difference is subtle, but the difference between success and failure usually *is* subtle. If you're prepared, then you're able to feel confident that you are capable of making the sale if it is possible to be made. Armed with this preparedness and confidence, you can then go into each selling situation hoping for the best, but realistically assuming the worst. You assume the worst simply because actual experience has proven the reality that no matter how well prepared you are, only a small percentage of deals actually close. The reason for this, obviously, is that there are an endless number of factors that are beyond your control. Using real estate as an example, certainly anyone who has ever tried to sell large properties knows that a deal can blow up over just about anything. There are unwanted third party opinions, a variety of ulterior motives, and all kinds of external factors beyond the control of the salesman.

Just as you can't manufacture a positive mental attitude, neither can you synthetically sustain one. I decided that the only way to guard myself against having my ego, self-image and belief shattered was to be mature and rational enough to acknowledge the reality that most deals simply do not close. I figured out that the only way I could sustain a true positive attitude—one that had been achieved through preparedness—was to realistically assume a negative result in any given sales situation. It worked, and it is still working for me today.

The very first year that I put my philosophy into action, my income skyrocketed to an almost unbelievable level ($849,901—which you'll be reading about in detail in the last section of this book), but it's important to understand that the handful of deals I closed during that first year represented only a small percentage of the total number that I worked on. Furthermore, it's significant to point out that I worked just as hard, and in many cases harder, on the scores of deals that *didn't* close as I did on the ones that resulted in income. Without firm belief in the Theory of Sustenance of a Positive Attitude Through the Assumption of a Negative Result, I would never have been able to continue trying after working so hard on each failure.

I guess you might say that it's somewhat of a paradox in that I prepared myself for long-term success by being prepared for short-term failure. I cannot emphasize enough that this works only if you're *prepared* to succeed; it doesn't work if you merely use it as an excuse to fail in a given situation where the factors are such that it is possible for you to succeed. To tell yourself that you assume you're going to fail in a certain deal—without being prepared and honestly confident that you'll succeed if the factors are within your control—is just as bad as standing in front of a mirror and telling yourself, without foundation, that you have a positive mental attitude.

With this theory in mind, I was able to look at each negative result as an educational experience which allowed me to extract the lessons learned, and then—and this is of key importance—forget about the negative result itself.

So much for positive mental attitude. Now as to "working hard, long hours," I initially recognized two important things:

First of all I came to the conclusion that the words "hard" and "long" are extremely relative. What one man considers to be working hard, another man may think of as loafing; what one man considers to be long hours may, by another man's standards, be very short hours. How could I allow myself to be bound by a success rule that was vague to the extent that it had no real meaning, a success rule that had no parameters, a success rule that could be adjusted to conform to one's own work habits, be they good or bad habits? Therefore, because of the relative nature of statements involving "working hard, long hours," I decided that not only could I not adhere to such rules, but, moreover, there was nothing to adhere *to*.

Since "working hard, long hours" is a relative phrase, it logically follows that there is no set number of hours per day that you have to work to succeed. The amount of time that you have to invest depends upon your individual ability and how much "success" you desire. A man with greater ability, who wants to earn $100,000 a year, might be able to do so by working four hours a day, while a man with lesser ability, who wants to earn $25,000 a year, might have to work ten hours a day to accomplish his objective. The "X" factor—the one thing that a man can do to cut his working time down to a minimum—is to work efficiently. And one of the most efficient things a man can do is to be selective as to the deals he works on. (Just as I pointed out with "sales situations," almost anything in life can be looked upon as a "deal.")

The second most basic thing about "working hard, long hours" is that it's almost axiomatic that there is a point of diminishing returns. The human body—and the human brain, in particular—can only be pushed so far before becoming run-down. How long a period your body can go without being recharged depends upon your physical makeup, but the fact remains that there is some point at which the results of effort expended begin to diminish; in fact, there's a point at which the results actually become negative. The surest way to become sloppy in your technique, and thus make costly errors, is to allow yourself to become mentally and physically fatigued.

Understanding that the phrase "working hard, long hours" is a relative one to begin with, and also realizing that the law of diminishing returns is a factor, my answer to the "hard work" myth became the

UNCLE GEORGE THEORY

The simplest way I know to explain this theory is to tell you, keeping relativity and diminishing returns in mind—and all other things being equal—that if you keep your nose to the grindstone and work hard, long hours, you're guaranteed to get only one thing in return: *Old!*

It doesn't take common sense or logic to understand this theory; all you need are your own two eyes. There's not a person in this world who hasn't seen the proof, with his own eyes, that working hard, long hours does not assure anyone of success.

I had an Uncle George who owned a corner grocery store and worked ten to fifteen hours a day all his life; he definitely succeeded in getting old, but he never got rich. This didn't take any great amount of insight on my part—only eyesight. I could see, with my own eyes, the kind of hours and effort the man put in during his lifetime, and I could also see that it never got him anywhere.

Everyone has an "Uncle George." He may not be an uncle in your case; he may be a cousin, a brother, or your own father, but you undoubtedly have an "Uncle George"—someone who has worked very hard over the years, played it square, kept his nose to the grindstone, yet never had any great financial success. Whenever you observed such a phenomenon, you were seeing the Uncle George Theory in action.

Is the world unjust? Maybe so, but I didn't lay down the framework of reality; I only learned to acknowledge it. The truth behind the Uncle George Theory isn't something that I invented; all I did was face the reality that it's a fact of life. I acknowledged this reality and made it work *for* me instead of allowing it to work against me.

I should conclude my discussion of the "hard, long hours" myth by noting that hard work will not *prevent* you from being successful, assuming you don't go beyond the point of diminishing returns. The Uncle George Theory only points out that hard work—aside from the fact that it's relative to begin with—will not, of and by itself, *assure* a person of success.

By removing the cornerstones of "success" mythology ("positive mental attitude" and "working hard, long hours"), I succeeded in clearing the site (my mind) where the unworkable structure (success

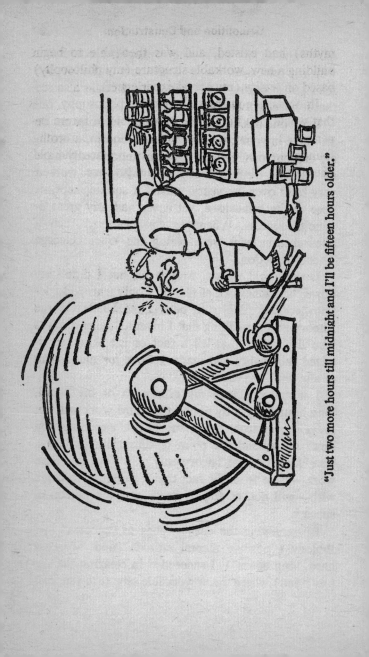

"Just two more hours till midnight and I'll be fifteen hours older."

myths) had existed, and was then able to begin building a new, workable structure (my philosophy) based on reality (my actual experiences).

In order to construct a workable philosophy, one that would stand up to the punishment of future experiences, I knew that I would have to have a strong foundation—new cornerstones to replace the old ones that had not worked in actual practice.

Chapter 2

Replacing The Myths

Translation: *What DOES work.*

The theories I discuss in this chapter are only a few of the many I developed in forming a workable philosophy over the years. There are five of them, to be exact, and they evolved over a period of time through repetition of experiences. I present them in a separate chapter, early in this book, because I think of them as the very foundation of my philosophy—the foundation upon which rest all of my other theories, including the Uncle George Theory and the Theory of Sustenance of a Positive Attitude Through the Assumption of a Negative Result.

I like to think of four of the theories in this chapter as the four cornerstones of my new, efficient, workable structure; these four theories are anchored to the fifth and most important theory, which I look upon as the bedrock of my entire philosophy. Without this "bedrock theory"—which I developed through simple observation and logic—I could never have constructed a workable philosophy. I will therefore begin the replacement of the "success" myths with the most basic theory of them all, the

THEORY OF REALITY

This theory emphasizes, first of all, that reality isn't the way you wish things to be, nor the way they appear to be, but the way they actually are. Secondly, the theory states that you either acknowledge reality and use it to your benefit or it will automatically work against you.

This sounds so elementary on the surface that you might wonder how it can possibly be the basis for my entire philosophy. All I can tell you is that—as obvious as you might think the above statements about reality to be—it's been my observation that most people pay lip service to reality but do not acknowledge it in actual practice. I don't like to expound on the reasons for the success or failure of others, but if I were forced to state an opinion as to what one single factor—from my personal observation—is most responsible for failure, my answer would have to be the inability to recognize and/or refusal to acknowledge reality.

Like most everyone else, I, too, went through all

of the normal idealistic phases. For many years I accepted the traditional brainwashing of society and confused the way I would have liked things to be with the way they really were. I will never cease to be amazed at the way I limped on, year after year, refusing to acknowledge reality in the face of one whipping after another. I feel very fortunate that my eyes eventually began to open.

I saw many people practice positive mental attitude exercises outlined in "success" books, only to go out and continue to fail. Their wish was that these exercises would work; the reality was that they didn't.

I did one altruistic good deed after another—concentrating on the other person's best interest—naively believing that my good deeds would be appreciated and that I'd be commensurately rewarded. At best I ended up with a handful of air; at worst I got a slap in the face. My wish was that I'd be appropriately rewarded; the reality was that I was not.

Like millions of people before me, I went into many deals on just a handshake—believing the other party's assurances when he told me that a handshake was all that I needed—only to have him end up beating me over the head. My wish was that I needed only the handshake; the reality was that I needed a clear, written agreement.

Year after year I listened to attorneys explain that they weren't "deal-killers"—that they weren't "typical attorneys" who concentrated on finding, rather than solving, problems—only to have those same attorneys end up killing one deal after another. My wish was that each new attorney who proclaimed himself to be "different" from other attorneys would not end up killing the deal; the reality was, with few exceptions, that most of these attorneys did end up trying to kill the deal.

In general, I, like most everyone else, wished that the game of business took place on a nursery school playground; the reality, however, was that the game of business is played in a vicious jungle. I decided that I must either accept that reality or, for my own well-being, get completely out of the game.

Reality is one category where, literally speaking, there is no limit to the number of examples I could give. I classify the above examples under the heading of: **Wish** versus **Reality.**

However, in addition to observing that people allow their wishes to become confused with reality, I also found that there was another factor that could blind a person to reality. That factor is illusion. I classify situations of this type under the heading of: **Illusion** versus **Reality.**

The best example I can think of is the market price of a stock. If a stock continues to rise at a rapid rate, the assumption that the company is doing well might be an illusion; the reality might be that some unknown entity is causing the stock price to rise for reasons completely unrelated to how well the company itself is doing. Obviously it's a lot harder to recognize and deal with illusions than wishes. I found, however, that as I became, through experience, more and more of a hard-nosed realist,

I also became skeptical and cynical enough to probe would-be illusions until I was able to strip them down to their hard realities.

Before going on to the four cornerstones of the new, workable philosophy, I'll again emphasize that the Theory of Reality is the very bedrock of that philosophy. All of the other theories you'll encounter in this book (including the key to winning —the Theory of Intimidation) are based on reality and were developed through actual experience, observation and analysis.

And now for the four cornerstones that sit upon that bedrock:

Cornerstone No. 1, the

THEORY OF RELATIVITY

This theory states, first of all, that few people take the trouble to consider facts in a relative light. Secondly, it emphasizes that you cannot logically decide upon a course of action (or inaction) with regard to anything unless it has first been carefully defined.

As with the Theory of Reality, the examples I could give are infinite:

Consider "honesty" for a moment. Without exception, everyone I've ever dealt with defines "honesty" to suit himself; everyone tailors his definition of "honesty" to conveniently fit his own actions. I've yet to meet a man who admits to being dishonest. Have you? On the other hand, have you ever *known* a dishonest man? I'm probably on pretty safe ground if I bet that your answer to the first question is negative and your answer to the second question is positive. Contradictions such as this one helped me to develop the Theory of Relativity.

Since I had dealt with many men whom I considered to be dishonest, yet had never known a man who had admitted to being dishonest, it was obvious that something was causing a tremendous gap. That gap was relativity. Each man interprets honesty— and everything else in life—in his own way. You do; I do; everyone you and I encounter does.

Once I acknowledged "honesty" as a subjective, relative thing, I realized that for years I had been operating under the delusion that there are only two types of people in the world: "honest" and "dishonest." I finally came to the realization that a person could only be "honest" or "dishonest" relative to the facts in a given situation or relative to some arbitrary set of standards. Therefore, if someone tells me that a person I'm dealing with is "dishonest," it's meaningless to me. I want him to carefully define what he means by "dishonest" in that particular situation so that I can then decide if the definition is relevant to my objective.

Another example is one that I touched upon in the first chapter when I referred to "working hard, long hours." As I pointed out, what's hard work to one man might be semi-retirement to another. You can only "work hard" relative to a given standard; are you working hard relative to how hard *you* usually work or relative to how hard *someone else* works? Again, phrases like "working hard, long hours" have no meaning to me unless they're clearly defined.

As a final example I point to the word "success." You can only be "successful" relative to some standard, whether that standard be someone else's achievements or your own goals. When a person talks to me about "success," I might (and usually do) have a completely different mental picture of what "success" means than he does. Standing alone, the word simply has no meaning; in order for us to have anything to discuss, I want him to define exactly what he's talking about when he refers to "success."

As with reality, it amazes me how many people fail to recognize and acknowledge relativity. They go through life allowing themselves to be constantly intimidated by vague words and statements that are meaningful only when examined in the light of their relativity.

Cornerstone No. 2, the

THEORY OF RELEVANCE

This theory states that no matter how interesting something is, no matter how true it is, or no matter how much it might please you, the primary factor to consider is whether or not it's relevant to what you're trying to accomplish. Secondly, it also states that it's important to work only on those things that you do recognize as being relevant.

In the old days I expended a lot of energy getting excited over things that proved to be a waste of time. I finally began to qualify everything by first asking myself whether or not it would help me to earn, and receive, income. If the answer was "no," then that "thing" wasn't relevant. As the years went by, I was constantly amazed at how much time people in the business world spend on irrelevant factors.

And this is certainly just as true in the real estate business as it is in any other field. In fact, once I became knowledgeable as to what the relevant factors in a real estate sale were, it became clear to me that the seller normally dwelled on qualities of his property that were *not* relevant in making a sale.

As an example, I found that one of the most common things a seller liked to emphasize was how much it had cost him to build his property. Did that fact cause me to have empathy for the seller? Yes, it did. But did that fact have an effect on the prospective buyer? No, it didn't. The seller's cost of construction simply wasn't relevant in the prospective buyer's determination of what the property was worth to him. If the seller spent twice as much money to build an apartment development as he should have, that wasn't the buyer's fault. The reality was that a buyer of income-producing properties was primarily interested in "cash flow," not building costs.

As a second example, a seller would often try to impress me with the fact that he was an "honest" guy and that I therefore needn't worry about my commission. A discussion of his honesty wasn't relevant; what *was* relevant was whether or not he was willing to put into writing our understanding regarding my commission. A discussion of "honesty," then, is not only relative, but it is also *irrelevant* when it comes to business dealings. Note that I did not say that honesty itself is not relevant in a business deal, but that a *discussion* of honesty is not relevant. In other words, parties to a transaction needn't waste their time trying to impress each other with their "honesty;" that is irrelevant. The time should be spent on putting their understanding in writing; a *written agreement* is relevant.

As a final illustration of the Theory of Relevance, if a seller wanted me to cut my commission because he hadn't realized how many additional expenses he was going to have at the closing, that—in my mind —wasn't relevant. I might have had empathy for the seller in such a situation, but that didn't make his problem relevant where my commission was concerned. It was no more relevant than if I had said that—because of some personal problems—I was in need of money and would therefore like my commission to be *higher* than the one we had agreed upon. What *was* relevant regarding my commission was what our written agreement said.

In becoming adept at recognizing what was and was not relevant, I found that it was not only important to try to keep other people in my deals from going off on irrelevant tangents, but that it was even more important to keep my own attention focused only on relevant factors. As a basic part of my philosophy, I became determined that I would not waste my time and effort on factors that were not relevant to my earning, and receiving, income. Simple, but important; simple, but practiced by very few people.

Cornerstone No. 3, the

THIRTY YEAR THEORY

Like all of my other theories, this one is firmly based on the bedrock of my philosophy—the Theory of Reality. The Thirty Year Theory has to do with death. I came to the conclusion that most people tend to block from their conscious minds the reality that they're going to die—and in a relatively short period of time, at that. I certainly didn't like facing that fact any more than does anyone else, but I finally did so after the Theory of Reality became firmly entrenched in my thinking. I simply recognized that death is a reality. I quit hiding my head in the would-be sands of eternal life and faced the reality that—give or take a few years—I had about thirty years left to "get on with it." Sure, I might stretch that to fifty years, but on the other hand circumstances might cut it down to one. Thirty was merely a "working number" I chose because it seemed to me at the time to be a reasonable estimation of how many years I had left to play the game of life, barring the unforeseen.

If there is something beyond our present earthly existence, that will be just great; but analyzing the only facts I had at my disposal, I decided that I had no way of knowing for certain whether or not there was anything beyond this life. I reasoned that I had better look at this time around as my only shot—just to play it safe—and consider anything that might come afterward as a bonus. I made up my mind that I was not going to lose—because of fright, intimidation or any other reason—what might be my only opportunity to play the game. I decided that if I only had about thirty years left, I had better go after all of the good things I could get as quickly as possible.

And that's the essence of the Thirty Year Theory: to go after all you can get, as quickly as you can get it, because you acknowledge the reality that your time for doing so is limited. When my participation in the game of life ends, I don't want to be caught begging for an extra inning—for one more chance to get some goodies. I've never known of a person who was given an extra inning, have you?

For obvious reasons, the Thirty Year Theory doesn't need examples—it speaks for itself. It's pretty final.

Cornerstone No. 4, the

ICE BALL THEORY

The simplest way to explain the Ice Ball Theory is to tell you that I came to the conclusion it was ridiculous to take myself too seriously, because years from now it wouldn't make any difference anyway.

At first blush it might seem to you that this is a contradiction to the Thirty Year Theory, but it definitely is not. In fact it goes hand-in-hand with that theory. The Ice Ball Theory eliminates ulcers and headaches and makes it possible to enjoy those last "thirty years" even when things aren't going exactly as you'd like them to. In the game of business, this attitude puts you at a decided advantage over opponents who tend to view every deal as life or death; consequently, they press for results at crucial moments when you, on the other hand, are able to calmly maintain your objectivity. And as you've seen many times through your own experience, the harder someone presses for a result, the less likely it is that he will obtain that result.

While the substance of this theory developed over a long period of time, I adopted the "ice ball" tag from something I once read in a science book. I happened to be reading a section which explained that the sun is slowly burning out and that in about 50 billion years there won't be any sun at all. According to the book, the earth will then be nothing but a "frozen ice ball." There was a horrifying illustration—an artist's conception—of what the earth might look like at that time.

My first instinct was fear. The explanation and illustration were done with such realism that they sent chills up my spine. My second instinct, however, was to laugh. It suddenly occurred to me that what I was reading was reality, that there was absolutely nothing I could do about it, and that, in light of this long-term reality, the immediate problems concerning me—particularly in the game of business—were so insignificant as to make me feel like an ant. I could not imagine how anything I was presently involved in could possibly matter 50 billion years from now when the earth was an ice ball.

This attitude (not to take myself too seriously because, in the final analysis, it wouldn't matter anyway) actually strengthened my feeling about the Thirty Year Theory. It made me look at life as a big game and at business as a sort of huge poker game within that bigger game of life. I thought of the earth as a giant poker table upon which the game of business is played, with only a fixed number of chips on the table. Each player gets to participate for an unknown period of time, and the name of the game is for him to see how many of the chips he can pile onto his stack. Of and by themselves, the chips, of course, are of no use to the player, but they *are* a means to an end; the rules of the bigger game of life provide for the exchange of these chips for those things that *help* to create the greatest amount of enjoyment in the player's remaining "thirty years."

You might ask, "If life is just a game, why play so hard to win?" To that I would answer, "Heck, if it *is* only a game, why *not* have some fun and try to win?"

I decided I would go for all I could get, as quickly as I could get it, while I still had the opportunity to play. Recognizing that both life and business are just games made it easy for me not to take myself too seriously and, consequently, made it easier to "win." After all, if it's just a game there's no sense in viewing each move as life or death; there's no reason to be afraid to be aggressive or take chances. The reality is that there's no way you're going to get out of this thing alive, anyway, so why play a conservative game?

And so ends the replacement of the myths . . .

In the next section I relate some of the horrors I encountered prior to having the Ice Ball Theory firmly implanted in my mind, and I also explain how they helped me to form my workable philosophy and the techniques for applying that philosophy to the earning, and receiving, of income in giant proportions. Had it not been for my early understanding of the Theory of Sustenance of a Positive Attitude Through the Assumption of a Negative Result, I would never have been able to survive the seemingly endless number of heartaches, humiliations and frustrations that I endured during those initial years of intense learning.

MY UNDERGRADUATE DAYS AT SCREW U.

Translation: Those Early Years
Of Learning Through Experience.

Chapter 3

My Qualifications For Entering
Screw U.

Translation: *Important knowledge I acquired prior to entering business.*

Although I was still wet behind the ears when I entered the real estate business and had no concept of the devastating realities that awaited me, I could never have survived if I hadn't already been armed with a couple of theories dating clear back to my "don't-even-know-which-end's-up" days (to keep things simple, I lump all high school and college students into this category since their ability to learn anything worthwhile is constantly being hampered by "formal education"). In fact, had I not learned certain basic, elementary lessons years earlier, I would have never even gone into the real estate business and most certainly would not have lasted more than a few weeks if I had.

What would have stopped me instantly was the discouragement of many people already in the business. It was interesting to note that on several occasions when I talked to other real estate salesmen about obtaining a real estate license, they went to great lengths to tell me how tough their profession was, how it was almost impossible to get started, how exceptional a man had to be to succeed as a real estate salesman, and, generally, why it would be a mistake for me to enter their field. Many years earlier this kind of talk would have totally intimidated me because I would have been convinced, based on these discouraging remarks, that I'd be wasting my time to even make the effort. Fortunately, however, I had paid some dues long before I ever reached the point where I was ready to enter the real estate business, so their remarks didn't bother me.

Based on previous experiences on a very elementary level, I decided that all members of the "Discouragement Fraternity" had one thing in common: they were full of baloney. It was my opinion—and still is—that a guy who tries to impress upon a newcomer how tough his business is, really is only attempting to bolster his own ego because of lack of actual accomplishment. It appeared to me that the more a person tried to discourage me from entering his field, the more insecure he was.

The two theories that helped me to survive my "entrance exam" (getting past the Discouragement Fraternity) at Screw U. (my early years in business) are the main subjects of this chapter. The first one is the

TORTOISE AND HARE THEORY

Let me explain it this way: Don't tell me how fast you get out of the starting blocks; I'm only interested in where you are when the race is over.

That says it all. So many people forget that it's a nine inning ball game. The guy who goes ahead in the first inning merely wins a battle; the guy who's ahead at the end of nine innings wins the war. In the games of life and business—as in any game—battles aren't relevant. Battles are for ego-trippers; wars are for money-grippers.

When I was still in my teens, I observed that although I was a very slow starter at just about everything I did, I always seemed to come on strong at the end. The only explanation I could think of as to why I started out so slowly was that I was a perfectionist by nature. I had to get all of the ground rules in order, have everything exactly defined, and get the complete lay of the land before I got going.

I finally began to jokingly compare myself to the fabled tortoise in the tortoise and hare tale. I always thought of myself as being—like the tortoise—basically unimpressive.

Clear back in my "don't-even-know-which-end's-up" days, I found that it was not so important to be the life of the party or the center of attention in a crowd. The important thing is what happens after the party is over; the real advancement is made when you go one-on-one with a person behind closed doors. I came to find that glibness in a crowd is just part of the "all show and no dough" syndrome.

Summing it up, I must admit that I wish I had the type of personality to be impressive on a first meeting and the mental aptitude to be a fast starter. The reality, though, is that I don't have these qualities, and even back in those early days I was able to recognize and acknowledge this reality. But since I do not have these qualities, I try to use what abilities I do have as effectively as possible. My motto has always been: "If you slow down enough to look over your right shoulder, I'll pass you on the left; if you slow down enough to look over your left shoulder, I'll pass you on the right; and if you slow down long enough to try to block my pass on either side, I'll jump over you, if necessary. You'd better keep your eyes straight ahead, because that sound you hear behind you is me . . . breathing down your neck."

After years of playing the role of the tortoise, I had survived too many early races to be intimidated by the Discouragement Fraternity when I entered the real estate business.

The other theory which protected me against the Discouragement Fraternity when I entered Screw U. is the

ORGANIC CHEMISTRY THEORY

Unlike the majority of my theories, this one grew out of a specific incident. When I was in the *other* kind of school (the one that keeps you in a state of "don't-even-know-which-end's-uppedness"), I took a course in organic chemistry. This particular course was purported to be the hardest subject of the school year, and, as best I can recall, something over half of the previous class had failed it. After the first lecture, I was convinced that I, too, was doomed to flunk organic chemistry. I had absolutely no idea what the instructor was talking about; for all I knew, a molecule could have been a spare part in an automobile engine.

The worst, however, was yet to come. The next day we had our first laboratory session, and it was like a psychedelic nightmare; all I could see was one big blur of test tubes, acid bottles and white aprons. I was so lost that I considered it to be a giant step forward when I finally found my way to my laboratory desk. I kept thinking and hoping that an instructor would appear at the front of the laboratory and explain what we should be doing, but it never happened. I thought that I must have accidentally missed out on some previous instructions about laboratory, and what really concerned me was that everyone else seemed to know exactly what they were doing.

Then I saw him—six-feet two, blond crew cut, and a look of self-assurance that suggested both boredom (with how easy it all was) and disdain (for those thickheads like me). As big as life, there he was, standing right at the end of my laboratory row —the guy who was to be the focal point of one of the greatest revelations of my life, a revelation that I was to transform into a permanent theory without which I could never have earned a dime's worth of income years later, long after my graduation from Screw U.

The guy at the end of that row was a "Court Holder." (Later I was to find that Court Holders come in all different shapes, sizes and colors. In ensuing years I encountered fat, short Court Holders with curly black hair; skinny, tall ones with silver-grey hair; medium weight, average height ones with red hair; every shape, size and color combination you can think of.)

Surely you know what a Court Holder is. Very simply, a Court Holder is a guy who makes a career out of holding court. You've met as many Court Holders as I have. You know—the guy at a cocktail party with one elbow on the mantle, a drink in his hand, and a group of information-starved puppies flocking around him in a semi-circle while he explains how utterly simple it all is. Above all, he is a champion intimidator.

A real Court Holder is not particular where he holds court, either. He can do it just as effectively in the clubhouse locker room, at the office, or, by golly, in a chemistry lab. Actually, the only requirement for him to call his court to session is that there be two or more information-starved puppies willing to become his subjects. The more subjects he has in his court, of course, the better he likes it; the more wide-eyed they are with awe, the more inspired the Court Holder is to sprinkle smatterings of his seemingly infinite knowledge around the court.

In chemistry lab, my eyes nearly bulged out of my head watching that fantastic kid flipping test tubes around nonchalantly, lighting his Bunsen burner backhanded, and leafing through his laboratory workbook so quickly it appeared he would finish the entire course in less than two days. The crowd was already gathering around him. Hope shot into my heart as I bounded down the aisle toward this veritable fountain of knowledge. Surely there must be a crumb or two of information he could spare a hopelessly lost soul like me; surely he would not turn me away cold.

I was in luck. As the Court Holder breezed through the laboratory experiments for that particular day, he simultaneously held court for a dozen or so puppies (and one tortoise). He even took the trouble to answer a couple of my questions (such as, "Where do I get a key to my locker?" and "Who do I see about getting a laboratory apron?") without so much as looking up from his test tubes. I wasn't even granted a look of disdain like most of the other subjects in his court; I guess I was so low in the society of organic chemistry that I was considered an untouchable.

This pattern went on for several weeks, and, even though I eventually succeeded in getting both an apron and a key to my locker, I finally accepted the fact that I would never be anything but an untouch-

"All right, all right . . . I'll try to explain how utterly simple it all is, but I only have about six hours to spare."

able in organic chemistry. Being a tortoise and not knowing any better, I did the only thing that I could under the circumstances. I trudged ahead, tortoise style, studying my textbook hour after hour each night. No matter how much I studied, though, I still never seemed to be up-to-date on what was being discussed in class and I continued to be completely lost in laboratory; no matter how much I studied, it seemed apparent that I would always be an untouchable in relation to the Court Holder.

Then one day, a funny thing happened on the way to court: we had an examination.

When the instructor passed out the blank test papers, you could hear moans throughout the room as the students began to glance at the questions. Much to my amazement, though, whatever had been going on in laboratory for the past several weeks evidently had also been explained in the textbook, because the material on the test seemed very familiar to me. When the exam was over, students came stumbling out of the classroom looking shell-shocked and talking in a thoroughly defeated manner. I was too embarrassed to even think of mentioning it, but frankly the questions had not seemed that difficult to me. Surely, I reasoned, I must have completely misunderstood the subject matter in my studying, or the test would have seemed hard to me, too.

When the test papers were handed back to us about a week later, you could feel the tension throughout the room. The instructor came before the class and announced the "curve" (grading scale based on averages) for the test. It went something like this:

48 and up	A	(excellent)
40-47	B	(good)
26-39	C	(average)
20-25	D	(poor)
19 and under	F	(failing)

The instructor said that the scores had ranged from zero to 105 (there had been two bonus questions, so it was theoretically possible to score 108 on the test), but out of a class of approximately 300 students, the next highest grade (after the score of 105) was a 58. Imagine: the second highest score in the class was 47 points less than the top grade!

The instructor said that it was only appropriate to hand back the paper with the astonishing score of 105 first, and that he would then call the rest of the students in alphabetical order to come up and get their test papers. The kids sitting around the Court Holder began patting him on the back and elbowing him ("You sonufagun, you . . ."), but he looked so bored by the certainty of it all that I thought he was going to fall asleep.

P.S. He should have. The Court Holder didn't get the 105; in fact, he didn't even get the 58. What this master intimidator did get was a good solid 33 that placed him in about the middle of the class.

By now you might have guessed who did get the 105. Yes sir, it was none other than The Tortoise himself. I was actually embarrassed when I walked up to the front of the room to get my paper. For most of the remaining hour I felt about 600 eyes staring at me. If eyes could speak, I guess they would have been saying, "Who in the hell is this Ringer guy, anyway? I've never even seen him in here before." When the bell rang, I hustled out the door, feeling too self-conscious to talk to anyone. I resigned from the court and breezed through the remainder of the course with a high "A." The only thing that made me uncomfortable the rest of the year was the feeling that the Court Holder was constantly glancing at me out of the corner of his eye during laboratory sessions.

Thank you, Court Holder, wherever you are. Since I encountered you, I've met your cousins, your brothers, your uncles, your nephews, and all of your other relatives, and in each case I was able, because of you, to instantly spot them as Court Holders. As a result I've been able to earn, and receive, a great deal of income because, after my experience with you, I was able to focus in on intimidation as the key to winning.

Would you like it summed up in simple definition form? Okay, what the Organic Chemistry Theory says is:

Don't allow yourself to be intimidated by know-it-alls who thrive on bestowing their knowledge on insecure people. Put cotton in your ears and blinders next to your eyes, and trudge ahead with the confidence that whether or not someone else "knows it all" isn't really relevant; the only thing that's relevant is what *you* know and what *you* do.

If the other guy wants to hold court, that's his business; you just mind your own. What someone else knows, or doesn't know, will not affect your success one way or another.

Thus, armed with the Tortoise and Hare Theory and the Organic Chemistry Theory, I was qualified to enter Screw U. They gave me the strength to withstand the negative barrages of intimidation directed at me by the Discouragement Fraternity and the courage to forge ahead into the real estate business.

Chapter 4

Three Unforgettable Professors
At Screw U.

Translation: *I learned that there are only three
types of people in the business world.*

I particularly like to refer to my first three years in
the real estate business as my "undergraduate days
at Screw U." because it was during that time that I
was forced, through brutal experience, to face the
realities of the business world. You might say that
my "major" subject was Reality and my "minor"
was Real Estate.

The most important reality I learned during those
three struggling years was that there are basically
only three types of people in the business world. It

was not until I acknowledged this reality that I was prepared to organize my philosophy into usable form and develop techniques for applying it to my specific objective.

It would take me more space than I have in this entire book to relate my experiences with every person I encountered during my undergraduate days at Screw U., so in the following three chapters I describe only three of the best remembered "professors" I learned from—professors who serve as stereotypes for the three kinds of people in the business world.

I firmly maintain that these three are the only types that exist, with one qualification: they do not include persons who stand to directly benefit as a result of your earning, and receiving, income. The latter type of exception is rare and will stand out like a sore thumb on those few occasions when it does exist.

Because it is appropriate to the theme of this book, I will give you a classic example of a person who does *not* stand to benefit as a direct result of your earning, and receiving, income. That example would be the seller of a property in a situation where you're the real estate salesman. (If you're not in the real estate business, forget that fact for a moment; what's important is the fundamental truth in the basic principle.) The goody-two-shoes fantasy that the seller will benefit by your "success" in such a situation is nothing more than the inability to recognize and/or refusal to acknowledge reality.

Remember, "success" is one of those extremely

relative words. The seller might benefit by your success in selling his property, but he won't benefit by your success in collecting a real estate commission. Where you're concerned, the latter (collecting a commission) should be your objective, and the former (selling his property) should be kept in its proper perspective: it is only a means to an end (receiving a commission).

Unfortunately, the myth that "the only way a deal works is if everybody's happy and 'benefits' by the transaction" was not intended to include real estate salesmen. The "everybody" in that fairy tale refers only to the buyer and seller; the reality is that the worse the salesman makes out, the better it is for the seller (and theoretically the buyer).

If you think about the above classic example for a moment, you might understand why certain people have been less than fair with you in past dealings, regardless of what type of business you're in. It might have been in their best interest to see you "succeed," but their definition of your success probably didn't include their having to pay you what you had earned.

In theory form, what I've been discussing here is the

THREE TYPE THEORY

What this theory states is that there are only three types of people who exist in the business world (again, with the one exception being a person who stands to directly benefit as a result of your earning, and receiving, income), as follows:

Type Number One:

This type lets you know from the outset—either through his words or actions, or both—that he's out to get all of your chips. He then follows through by attempting to do just that.

Type Number Two:

This type assures you that he's not interested in getting your chips, and he usually infers that he wants to see you get everything "that's coming to you." He then follows through, just like Type Number One, and attempts to grab all of your chips anyway.

Type Number Three:

This type also assures you that he's not interested in getting any of your chips, but, unlike Type Number Two, he sincerely means it. That, however, is where the difference ends; due to any one of a number of reasons—ranging from his own bungling to his personal standards for rationalizing what's right and wrong—he, like Types Number One and Two, still ends up trying to grab your chips.

In summation, I realized that no matter how a guy came on, he would, in the final analysis, attempt to grab all of my chips (again with the one exception that I pointed out).

It made sense that if the name of the game was to see how many chips a player could stack on his pile, then no one was going to want me to receive any chips unless by doing so he would also get more for himself. Or, in even simpler language: In business, no one ever does anything for anybody else without expecting to gain something in return. A person may say that he's doing something just to be nice— and he may even believe it—but don't *you* believe it. In the final analysis, his non-altruistic subconscious mind will automatically regulate his actions.

Again, I'm not saying that I *wish* everyone in the business world fell into these three categories. What I *am* saying is that my firsthand experiences at Screw U.—and all of my observations since then— have proven to me that it's simply one of the realities of the business world.

Recognizing the three types of people who exist in the business world is such an integral part of my philosophy that I've set aside the next three chapters to discuss three of my stereotype "professors" at Screw U.—those proctologists who did such an excellent job of teaching me how to recognize the members of their species.

Chapter 5

I Really Didn't Mean To Cut Off Your Hand At The Wrist, But I Had No Choice When You Reached For Your Chips

Translation: *Type Number Three is sincerely sorry, but the result is just the same as if he were glad.*

What makes Type Number Three so deadly is that he's neither menacing like Type Number One, nor diabolical like Type Number Two; his intentions are good. He *wants* to see you get a "fair shake," but because of the reality of the laws of non-altruism he is "forced," by any one of a number of "reasons," to attempt to grab your chips. Because he is really and truly sorry for having to hurt you, it's very difficult to reach the level of sophistication where you're able to view a Type Number Three as a dangerous opponent in the game of business.

I encountered a Type Number Three on my very first day at Screw U.—my initial day in the real estate business. At that time I knew almost nothing about real estate, let alone the complicated psyches of buyers and sellers. Yet, strictly by chance, the first deal I worked on was very large—a $5 million apartment development in Cincinnati. I had heard rumors that the owners of this project, which was still partly under construction, were in serious financial trouble, so I contacted one of them and asked him for a job.

I told him that I would like to work on solving the financial problems regarding his Cincinnati apartment development, but he was negative. He said he could not afford me, and also pointed out that I had no previous experience in the real estate business. I assured him that I could make up in energy, enthusiasm and creativity what I lacked in knowledge and experience, but he still refused to hire me. Being the ever persistent tortoise, I didn't let it go at that. I finally offered to work for this man on a "prove it or else" basis: I told him that I would work without a guaranteed salary and would even pay my own expenses, but that if I solved his financial problems in Cincinnati I wanted to be paid handsomely in return. This was an offer he couldn't refuse, so, on the strength of that shaky understanding, my real estate career began.

Unintentionally, I was applying the law of risk-return: the greater the guarantee, the lower the potential return; the higher the risk, the higher the potential return. (The latter is really what being a salesman is all about; ideally a salesman should have no guarantees, but also no limit on what he can earn.) If this man—the first professor I encountered at Screw U.—had agreed to put me on his payroll, I doubt that it would have been for more than $150 a week. As it turned out, however, I ended up making $6,500 for just three months' work. That kind of money in such a short span of time had been beyond my comprehension in previous years.

Looking back in retrospect and realizing how valuable my experience with this professor later turned out to be, I would have to say that on a value-for-value basis I probably should have paid *him* for all of the experience and knowledge I acquired during the time I worked on his problems, rather than the other way around.

Once I started to work, I found that the problems centered around the fact that the principals had undertaken the venture, as is so often the case, with little or no cash of their own up front. If you're at all familiar with real estate, you know that most developers always have it "figured out" (usually very unrealistically) that they can either "finance out" in building a project or, through some fancy footwork, somehow see it through to completion and eventually pay all of the accrued construction debts through "cash flow."

The gentleman I went to work for had a partner in this particular deal, and, as is par for the course when ventures don't work out, he was not on good terms with him. His partner lived in Cincinnati and was what you might call the "working partner;" he was actually on the construction site every day, directing the development of the project. My "employer" did not live in Cincinnati, and his primary involvement had been in originally putting the deal together. I therefore decided that I had better go to Cincinnati and talk directly with the working partner since he would probably have a more current grasp of the facts.

And what an experience that turned out to be. There's no way that I can ever begin to relate the humiliation and frustration I endured in trying to talk to the Cincinnati partner. On several occasions I set up definite appointments with this man, traveled all the way to Cincinnati, then sat in his waiting room for as long as eight hours. I did not fully understand it at the time, but he was a master intimidator.

I can remember one day in particular when I had a firm appointment with him at 9:00 a.m. and, just to be on the safe side, showed up at 8:45. Not only did he not even acknowledge my presence all morning, but around noon he bolted out of his office door with two other men and hurried right past me

—without even a nod—on his way to lunch. Out of desperation I called out to him and asked when he would be ready to meet with me. Not even breaking stride, and barely looking back over his shoulder, he mumbled something about "being back in a little while."

When I had occasion to recall that horrible day a few years later, I found it hard to believe that I had actually sat there like an idiot and allowed someone to so blatantly intimidate me—to treat me like just another piece of furniture in his reception room. You must remember, however, that at the time this occurred, it not only was the first real estate deal I had ever worked on, but in addition I was completely broke, had no other deals in the hopper, and had no idea of how to go about finding other deals. You might say that at that particular time it was the only game in town. Because of that fact I could not even afford to take a chance on going out and grabbing a sandwich for lunch. I didn't know when the Cincinnati partner might return to his office, and after waiting all morning I didn't want there to be any possibility of missing him when he did return.

When he finally showed up two hours later, I was a very stiff, very hungry, and very tired tortoise—so tired that I almost didn't look up in time to see him before he got to his office door. This time I called out in a much weaker, much more defeated voice, and this time he didn't even bother to look back. As his office door slammed shut, the thought of giving up the whole mess entered my mind, but fortunately the tortoise within me persisted; believe it or not I sat there until 5:00 p.m. I finally got to talk to the man only because, in desperation, I actually lunged in front of his path as he was leaving his office for the day.

Unbeknownst to me at the time, what I was experiencing were the horrors a man encounters when dealing from an inferior posture. (Years later, as you'll see in Chapter 9, experiences such as this one helped me to develop a theory which formed the basis for many of the techniques I used in applying my philosophy to my own particular objective.)

After a series of punishing meetings like the one above, the gist of what I learned from the Cincinnati partner was that he had talked a mortgage banker into increasing the construction loan on the project and immediately advancing some additional funds, providing certain conditions were met. He told me that in order to make this deal with the mortgage banker, however, there were complications that would practically require him to buy out his "nonworking" partner's interest in the development. He gave me a purchase price that he thought he could live with, whereupon I told him that I would discuss it with my "employer" (the nonworking partner).

I then went back and explained the situation to the nonworking partner, but I "packaged" it a little differently; I did not relay it as an "offer." The reason I phrased the Cincinnati partner's proposal a little differently was because not only was my understanding with the nonworking partner not in writing, but we did not even have a verbal agreement as to the exact amount of the fee I was to receive or even what I had to do to receive it. I was just supposed to "be paid handsomely" if I "solved his financial problems" in Cincinnati. Although I had just entered Screw U., it was obvious to me that it was time to be more definitive.

I reasoned that if I told the nonworking partner that his Cincinnati partner was already prepared to pay the price he had just indicated to me, and if it were acceptable to the nonworking partner, then he would no longer need me to make the deal. Furthermore, once he knew what the offer was, he was in a position to dictate to me what my reward should be.

I therefore told the nonworking partner that I had been "talking and negotiating" with his Cincinnati partner and, although I thought it would be extremely difficult, there was a chance that I might be able to get his partner to buy him out at a price that would get him off the hook for most of the debts he had incurred as a result of the Cincinnati venture.

But that wasn't the only way I repackaged the proposal. From what I knew of the mathematics of the project, I also recognized that the price the Cincinnati partner had quoted me was so low that it would probably only succeed in making the nonworking partner mad. Based on what he had told me about the extent of his monetary problems, I knew it was doubtful that the suggested buy-out price would completely bail the nonworking partner out of his financial difficulties, so I quoted him an even *lower* price than the one the Cincinnati partner had suggested, indicating that this was probably the best I could hope to do. The psychology involved was simply that I assumed he would want to negotiate the price upward no matter what the initial figure was that I quoted him, so I was hoping to negotiate up *to* the Cincinnati partner's suggested price rather than negotiate upward *from* that price.

His first reaction, of course, was that the price I had suggested was ridiculous. After several days of discussion, however, and many persistent and persuasive tortoise remarks later, the upshot was that I finally got the nonworking partner to understand that, in the long run, it would be better for him if I could get his Cincinnati partner to buy him out at a price roughly equal to the one that (unbeknownst to him) the Cincinnati partner had already indicated he was willing to pay. I convinced the nonworking partner that, as construction progressed, the project was destined only to get into deeper financial trouble than it was already in (which turned out to be exactly the case) and that he would be much better off to bail out now, get off the hook for any personal liability he had with regard to the project, and still manage to come up with enough cash to pay off at least a considerable number of his other debts.

You'll notice that I said I got him to agree to a price "roughly" equal to the one the Cincinnati partner had already verbally offered. I used that word purposely because what I really did was to work backward from the Cincinnati partner's suggested price and shoot for a figure that was about $6,500 lower than that price; the $6,500 represented an arbitrary figure I had picked as the amount I wanted to receive as my "problem solving" fee. I then told the nonworking partner that I would try to increase the price he had tentatively agreed to (once again I point out that this was an amount exactly $6,500 *lower* than the offer the Cincinnati partner had made) by "five to ten thousand dollars" so that I could "get a little something out of the deal, too." To that he nodded his head affirmatively; after all, anything I got "over and above" what he was getting really wasn't his anyway, right? Wrong! The reality, of course, was that the whole situation—as is the case with all commissions—was purely academic; it was strictly a matter of packaging. This is a good example of "Illusion versus Reality." By being a little imaginative I was able to create the illusion that whatever I got as a fee was "over and above" what he was getting; the reality was that the less I received as a fee, the more money the nonworking partner would get.

Although I was quite meek about it since it was my first such experience, I asked him if he would sign a simple document saying that the figure we had discussed was one that he agreed to accept from his Cincinnati partner for the purchase of his interest in the project. I told him that I just wanted to "have something in my hand" to show his Cincinnati partner when I tried to "persuade" him to "agree" to the deal. Phrasing is everything—my real purpose for having him sign such a paper, of course, was not just to "have something in my hand" when I went to Cincinnati, but to have something in writing regarding my fee. I told him that I would use $6,500 as a "working number" for my fee, tack it on to the figure he and I had discussed, then put the total figure into the document as the price he had agreed to accept from the Cincinnati partner.

To make it appear almost as an afterthought, I put the sentence about my $6,500 fee near the bottom of the document. In later years I realized that my instincts, even at that early point in my undergraduate days at Screw U., had been very good, because over and over again I was to find that "afterthought" is a pretty accurate representation of the way most sellers view a salesman's commission.

Subsequent to the nonworking partner signing the document, I went back to the Cincinnati partner and told him that I had gone through absolute hell (which was true) in trying to persuade his nonworking partner that the buy-out figure he had suggested to me was a good one. (I should emphasize once again that I really believed I was acting in the nonworking partner's best interest, because after studying all of the facts I felt sure in my own mind that he would only get into further financial trouble as construction of the project developed.) I indicated that

I had finally succeeded in making the nonworking partner see the light, but I did not show the Cincinnati partner the document the nonworking partner had signed.

And you've probably already figured out why. Just as I had packaged my presentation of the deal in such a way that the nonworking partner would think of my fee as "over and above" what he was getting, I also had to be sure that the Cincinnati partner didn't get any ideas about being able to "save" $6,500 by merely changing the original price (the one he had suggested to me) to a price equal to the net figure the nonworking partner had agreed to accept. As far as the Cincinnati partner knew, the original price he had discussed with me (which I again point out was an amount equal to the price the nonworking partner had agreed to accept *plus* my $6,500 fee) was the one his nonworking partner was willing to take.

I emphasized to the Cincinnati partner that his nonworking partner was, at best, uneasy about the proposed deal (which was also true) and that I could not guarantee he wouldn't change his mind if we didn't proceed with a closing rather promptly. At that point I had his attention and cooperation because his greed instinct had taken over. The Cincinnati partner, feeling that perhaps it was a one-time-only opportunity to get his nonworking partner out of the deal at a price he considered to be a bargain, did everything possible to help effect a quick closing. Naturally, though, when I went back to the nonworking partner I dramatized how hard it had been for me to get his Cincinnati partner to "agree" to the total figure (the one that included my $6,500 fee) stated in our document. I then indicated to him that I didn't know how long I could keep the Cincinnati partner committed to such a deal, and urged the nonworking partner to therefore do everything possible to effect a quick closing.

I then had a perfect situation set up: all three parties involved—the buyer, the seller and the "salesman" (technically, I guess I would be more correctly classified as a "consultant" in this particular deal) —were working hard to accomplish the same objective. As I said, I was acting only on raw instinct, and there's no question that I was lucky. That early in the game I had no idea of why I was doing the things I did; they just happened to turn out to be correct.

Before I go any further in describing the events surrounding my first experience at Screw U., I feel it necessary to deviate for just a moment. It occurs to me that this early in my book you may not be completely tuned in to the fundamentals of my philosophy (particularly the Theory of Reality). You may therefore be questioning whether my "creativity" in handling the delicate negotiations in Cincinnati was "proper" (by some arbitrary standard you may be using). In that regard I'll point out three things:

1) First of all, not only did I not originally have a written agreement with the nonworking

partner, but I did not even have a definitive verbal agreement. The entire situation was very vague; I had just volunteered to try to "solve his financial problems in Cincinnati," and, if "successful" in doing so, was supposed to "be paid handsomely in return." In other words there was no agreement, written or otherwise, that indicated it was my duty to present the nonworking partner with offers to buy out his interest in the property.

2) Secondly, the fact remains that what I did was indeed in the nonworking partner's best interest, as later events proved. As I said, after analyzing the situation I was convinced that the project was destined for further financial trouble, and this turned out to be exactly the case. Understanding the nonworking partner's unrealistic type of personality, I knew I couldn't work the deal out if I just presented him the Cincinnati partner's "offer" in a straightforward manner. But by being a little creative I believe I averted what would have been a total financial catastrophe for him later on, and the bottom line—which is really all that counts—is that both partners ended up being satisfied.

3) Thirdly—and most important from the standpoint of the contents of this book—is that the events at the closing (which I'm about to describe) proved that I had every reason to be cautious in how I handled the negotiations. When it got down to the short strokes, the nonworking partner's actions convinced me that I would have walked away from the closing without a dime if I hadn't gone out of my way to protect my own interest as well as his.

Now back to the action . . .

As we progressed toward a closing, I observed day by day a phenomenon that I was later to discover occurs prior to most real estate closings. The nonworking partner "sharpened his pencil" and continued to find one cost after another and one debt after another that he either had not previously considered or hadn't known about.

It is appropriate at this time to point out that the nonworking partner was an ultra-typical Type Number Three. Everyone who had ever dealt with him seemed to feel that he was really an "honest" guy and a "nice" person, but that he had experienced an excess of bad luck which had unintentionally caused him to damage many other people in addition to himself. So even though I didn't understand at that time what a Type Number Three was, the nonworking partner served as the professor for my first course at Screw U.

The closer we got to the closing, the more he sharpened his pencil. Being a Type Number Three, he was very nice and never came right out and said that he did not intend to pay my fee; he just mumbled a lot of negatives. The more figuring he did, the more he mumbled, and the more concerned I became. I finally became so worried that I asked myself a question only someone as slow and inexperienced as me would have dared to ask. That question was: "If the buyer and seller in a real estate deal are represented by attorneys at a closing, why shouldn't the middleman (salesman, finder, consultant, or whatever) also be?" After all, didn't I have a vested interest in the deal, too?

But every time this question crossed my mind I told myself that if I showed up at the closing with an attorney, the nonworking partner would take it as such an insult to his "integrity" that he would probably refuse to pay me anything at all just on general principles. I was really intimidated, and that—as you'll see in later chapters—is the key to receiving, or not receiving, what you earn (not just in business, but in *all* of life).

Finally, the day of my first real estate closing arrived. I talked to the nonworking partner just a couple of hours before the closing was scheduled to take place, and in typical Type Number Three fashion he expressed sincere concern for my position. He said he felt terrible about it, but after adding up all the figures there was no way that he could spare even $100 out of the proceeds of the closing, let alone $6,500. I wondered to myself how he could talk in terms of his "sparing" when technically it was not even his money to spare; it occurred to me that those were *my* chips that he was indicating he couldn't "spare." It also occurred to me that the fact he felt bad about it was not really relevant. You can see, even at this early stage of my studies at Screw U., how my philosophy was beginning to take shape through actual experience.

The nonworking partner then assured me that in the not-too-distant future he would "see to it" that I got every dime that was "coming to me." He said he was working on many deals (all pie-in-the-sky I might add) which he expected to close soon, and that he would therefore have plenty of cash in the near future (more typical pie-in-the-sky talk).

The lucky thing for me was that I was stone broke. If I had been in a financial position to wait a few months, or even a few weeks, I would have undoubtedly backed off because I was still at a very intimidatable stage of my development. Consequently I acted out of sheer desperation; I was so pushed to the wall that I could not even wait another day, let alone weeks or months. However, I didn't say anything menacing to my "employer" because I did not want to put him on guard ahead of time. So in response to the "concern" he expressed, I just mumbled that I would see him at the closing and that "perhaps there might be a way to work something out."

I then made a monumental decision. I scurried over to the office of an attorney friend of mine, showed him the document the nonworking partner had signed, described the conversation I had just had with the nonworking partner, and told him that the closing was about to take place. The attorney and I then went over to the office of the nonworking partner's lawyer and found that all of the parties were already there preparing for the closing.

My attorney sat down with the other two lawyers, and the three of them went through the mechanics of finalizing the deal. Although I didn't understand the principle at the time, what I had going for me was the fact that there is an unwritten, universally accepted understanding among all attorneys. I call it the unwritten **Universal Attorney-to-Attorney Respect Law**. (I guess the simplest way to illustrate this law is to remind you of the last time you were a party to a lawsuit, and how the attorneys for both sides—notwithstanding the facts involved in the case—left the courtroom arm-in-arm discussing their upcoming Sunday golf game.) While the attorneys proceeded with the closing, I chatted with the two partners about the weather and other equally relevant subjects. Although I felt embarrassed, I tried to convey a very matter-of-fact attitude: Why *shouldn't* the "third party" to a closing also be represented by an attorney? After all, I was too inexperienced to know any better . . . wasn't I?

P.S. I got my $6,500 fee—at the closing.

How fortunate I was. I had learned firsthand about the deadliness of Type Number Threes, and had managed to do so without even getting burned. If I hadn't been so lucky, it's very possible that because of my financial situation I might not have been able to continue in the real estate business.

And in addition to the fact that my first professor taught me how a Type Number Three operates, I also received a bonus in that I got an answer to my naive question of: "Why shouldn't a salesman also be represented by an attorney at closings?" My actual experience had proven to me that the answer was an emphatic: *"He should!"* It's simply a matter of not being intimidated into thinking that you aren't entitled to the same rights as "principles."

. . . so I survived my first encounter with a Type Number Three by the skin of my teeth.

. . . and to boot, it was a classic example of earning while learning.

Chapter 6

I Really Meant To Cut Off Your Hand At The Wrist, And Before You Reached For Your Chips You Should Have Remembered My Warning

Translation: *Type Number One isn't sorry, because he warned you ahead of time how he plays the game.*

My second professor at Screw U. was a Type Number One, and again, as luck would have it, I was able to learn from him without being a casualty of his method of operation.

Before getting into a discussion of my experiences with my Type Number One professor, I should point out that although I wasn't aware of it I was already familiar with this type even prior to my entering Screw U. In fact, everyone in the world is familiar with Type Number One; it's just that people refer to Type Number One by other names—such as "crook," "bastard" or, even more vaguely, "bad guy." ("Crook," "bastard" or "bad guy" relative to what standard, or to whom?)

Since Type Number One wears a black hat, he's very easy to spot. Whether intentionally or otherwise, he makes it clear that he is out to pile as many chips as possible onto his stack, that his sole purpose is to win the game, and that anyone who attempts to grab any chips automatically becomes his opponent. In many respects he's not very clever since he lays his cards right on the table before the game even begins.

So prior to my experiences at Screw U. I did not realize that a Type Number One not only isn't "crooked," but in fact is the most "honest" (by my standard—"straightforwardness") of the three types of people who exist in the business world. This is in direct opposition to the brainwashing society had always given me, like everyone else, about Type Number One. If a Type Number One's menacing gestures scare you, it's your prerogative to simply avoid dealing with him in the first place. On the other hand, if you go into any sort of business transaction with a Type Number One, you go in with your eyes wide open. If you get burned, it's probably because you either did not face the realities involved

or you weren't prepared, but not because you were
sucked in under the guise that you were dealing with
someone whom you could "trust."

I would describe my relationship to my Type
Number One professor as a sort of "freelance employee." Because I was on his side of the fence I was
able to observe—at close range—how he operated,
without being on the receiving end of his blows. He
was a good professor to learn from because he was a
very successful Type Number One. He had accu-
mulated tremendous wealth through his vast knowledge of the real estate business.

This particular professor was in his late sixties
when I first met him. He was as hard as nails and
could be as mean as cat dirt when the going got
tough. He looked at the real estate business as one
big game, and, almost naively, seemed to assume
that everyone else was also playing the game just for
the thrill of winning. At his age and with his wealth,
he certainly didn't need any more chips for the purpose of obtaining material comfort, so it was purely
the fun—the enjoyment of winning—that attracted
him. (Just so there's no misunderstanding, however,
"winning" *means* getting as many chips as possible.
The *nature* of the chips, of course, is determined by
individual objectives and can take many forms—
such as money, trophies, or the love of another person—in fact, an infinite number of forms.)

As I recall, I first ran across his name, strictly by
chance, while looking through a "capital sources"
book. It was one of those examples of being in the
right place at the right time, but—and I emphasize

this—it would not have happened if I hadn't taken the initiative to obtain that book, study it, and then contact many of the sources it listed.

After being at Screw U. for several months I had begun to see that there was a tremendous need among builders for secondary financing. It appeared to me that this was an area of the business where I could secure an endless number of deals to work on, and I was looking through the "capital sources" book in an effort to find some second mortgage lenders, one of whom turned out to be my elderly Type Number One professor. He specialized in making large second mortgage loans on income-producing properties like apartment developments, shopping centers and office buildings.

He was a stern teacher who often tongue-lashed me for being too careless or too trusting. Whenever my inclination was to give a person the benefit of the doubt, his position was that there was no such a thing as "benefit of the doubt" in business dealings. His approach was to tie the other guy's hands behind his back, bind his feet, close off all exits of escape, and then "negotiate."

It was through this Type Number One that I first learned about the ace-in-the-hole that all wealthy people have in business dealings: staying power. I marveled at the fact that he was always prepared to walk away from any deal because there was no one deal that was life or death to him. As a result it was simply impossible to intimidate my professor.

The first deal he and I ever made together was a typical example of his modus operandi. I had brought him a $150,000 second mortgage loan application from a rather desperate builder who was willing to put up nine small apartment properties as collateral (subject, of course, to the first mortgage loans on the properties). My professor expressed an immediate interest in making the loan, and when I relayed that fact to the prospective borrower he became very anxious for the professor to inspect his properties.

That set the stage for the application of intimidation: the prospective borrower was anxious; my Type Number One professor was not.

When he finally came in to inspect the properties, the lender (my professor) shook his head and indicated that he would need more collateral in order to make the loan. The prospective borrower protested, insisting that the nine properties he was willing to give as security constituted excessive collateral to begin with. Enter intimidation: my professor thanked him for his trouble and indicated that he was going to fly back to New York; the prospective borrower—desperate for cash—quickly backed off and agreed to give him, as additional collateral, a first mortgage on a ten acre parcel of land that he said was going to be rezoned to an industrial classification very soon.

My professor not only took the land as additional collateral, but, as we got nearer the closing, insisted on inserting a clause in the loan agreement which stated that if the land was not, in fact, rezoned "industrial" at the end of one year, then he (the lender) could require that the borrower pay off an additional $20,000 on the principal of the loan. I thought to myself that this was a rather harsh condition, particularly since it appeared that the nine apartment properties alone were more than enough collateral in the first place. As it turned out, however, I hadn't seen anything yet; his greatest moves were still to come.

Just when it looked as though all of the details for a closing had been worked out and the borrower was becoming extremely anxious, my professor—"after reviewing the figures very carefully"—told him there was no way he could make a $150,000 loan based on the collateral they had been discussing; he said that $100,000 was the top figure he was willing to go. The borrower then became downright hostile. He emphatically refused to agree to the change, so once again my professor thanked him for his time and indicated he had better things to work on . . . and once again the borrower limped back to the "negotiating table." They finally "compromised" at $105,000.

By this time the borrower was beside himself with desperation, and, as you might have suspected, that fact did not go unnoticed by my lending professor. Before he was through he took advantage of his intimidating posture to land two final blows. For starters he required that the borrower "deposit" with him (the lender), each month, one-twelfth of the annual real estate taxes on the various properties—meaning that the professor would have the use of the borrower's tax money until the real estate taxes were actually due, rather than allowing the borrower to have the use of these funds.

The final blow, however, was the real coup de grace. When the old Type Number One examined the "rent rolls" for each of the properties, he noticed that one of them—the construction of which had just been completed—still had a considerable number of vacancies. He insisted that $20,000 out of the $105,000 loan be retained by him until that property reached an occupancy rate of approximately 80%. The same objections, the same gestures, the same result. Intimidation was the deciding factor: the borrower ended up agreeing to all of the professor's conditions.

Looking back on that deal now, I realize it was just a matter of at what point the lender decided to show mercy. He had the goodies; the borrower was desperate. He had staying power; the borrower was running out of time. He was intimidating; the borrower was intimidated. It was the old Type Number One's kind of deal: totally one-sided. Believe it or not, he did finally show mercy and we succeeded in closing the loan. I received a nominal fee while being able to observe, at close range, how one of the great Type Number Ones in history operated.

As the professor and I walked out of the building where the closing had taken place, I told him that the borrower seemed like a "nice guy" and I therefore hoped he would be able to abide by all of the conditions in the loan agreement. The professor replied that that wouldn't be possible. I was puzzled and asked him to explain what he meant by that statement, whereupon he smiled and said, "If you take the trouble to read the loan agreement carefully, you'll see that he was technically in default the moment he signed it."

Now *that's* what you call a practical course at Screw U.

In the months that followed, the old man began taking a personal liking to me—I suppose because of my persistence and attention to detail, and no doubt because he appreciated my straightforward manner. I was extremely neat and accurate in obtaining and putting into presentation form all of the facts regarding the deals I brought to him. If additional information was needed in order to proceed further, I obtained it immediately even if it meant flying a thousand miles at my own expense to secure those facts.

He recognized—because of his position as a lender and my abilities as a finder—that it was in his best interest to see me make money. He was smart enough to understand that my making money would encourage me to continue working hard to bring him the best deals possible. So even though he was an orthodox Type Number One in situations where it was not in his best interest to see the other guy make money, he qualified as one of those rare exceptions—in relation to me—in that my earning income was of benefit to him in the long run.

Furthermore, because it was also in my best interest to see *him* make money, I went out of my way to protect my professor in every deal. To many of our "clients" I became cynically known as his watchdog; if there was one thing I recognized even then, it was which side my bread was buttered on. The old man and I had a wonderful relationship because it was based on the most honest (again, by my standard—"straightforwardness") foundation any business relationship can have: the Profit Motive.

As mean as he was to me at times, I not only obtained great knowledge from him, but I actually grew fond of the old guy; I really respected him for his candid approach. I would hate to think how much longer it might have taken me to learn many of the realities of the business-world jungle had I not had the opportunity to work closely with this aged Type Number One professor for a couple of years.

Chapter 7

I Really Meant To Cut Off Your Hand At The Wrist When You Reached For Your Chips, Even Though I Had Assured You That Was Never My Intention

Translation: *Type Number Two isn't sorry, because—in spite of what he may have told you —he never intended for you to get any goodies in the first place.*

There were several turning points in my career, but the biggest one, by far and away, was the experience that I'm going to describe for you in this chapter. In fact, until a person learns how to recognize and deal with a Type Number Two, it's extremely difficult for him to make any significant progress in the game of business. As I've already pointed out, a Type Number One can be easily spotted and, therefore, defended against. As to a Type Number Three, because of his sincerity and normally easygoing manner, his actions can be legally offset without too much trouble. But a Type Number Two is just plain treacherous. He is both hard to recognize and extremely difficult to handle. He often gives the outward appearance of being a Type Number Three, and he can sometimes even pass for a Type Number One, but the thing that all Type Number Twos have in common is that they're devious; they work hard at trying to get your chips.

It was not until I had completed the course with my Type Number Two professor at Screw U. that I began making preparations to graduate on to bigger and better things. Not that I had never encountered a Type Number Two before, but, as with the other two types, I had not recognized the people who fell into this category for what they really were; nor had I ever studied or analyzed the methods used by a Type Number Two. My Type Number Two professor at Screw U. was a great teacher because—like the two professors before him—he was an extreme illustration of his species. In fact I have never run across a more classic example of a Type Number Two, nor have I since been involved in any situation that better illustrated how a Type Number Two operates.

One day when I was making "cold" phone calls in an effort to solicit new second mortgage deals, I happened to contact the head of an apartment development company which purportedly owned several large apartment projects. He expressed an interest in talking further with me, so I made an appointment to see him.

When I went to his office for our first face-to-face discussion I was totally impressed. Although within a year I would view his operation as strictly run-of-the-mill, at that stage of my education I was completely intimidated. He spent a great deal of time expounding on the virtues of dealing only with people who had reputations for being "honest"—people of "integrity" like himself. And he wasn't shy about tossing around the names of competitors whom "everyone knew were less than scrupulous." (Later I was to learn that this kind of talk is a dead giveaway for a Type Number Two.)

Talk about "holier than thou," my new mentor really laid it on heavy. And talk about gullible, this tortoise ate up every word. I sat there like a dummy, nodding my head in agreement with such statements as, "Life is too short to deal with people who aren't honorable." I "oohed" and "aahed" as he further impressed me by dropping the names of big institutions which had either financed some of his projects or wanted to back him on future developments. Man, he was wearing a white hat so tall it nearly touched the ceiling.

When we finally got down to talking about the

"It's important to deal only with people of integrity—like me, for example."

business at hand, he indicated that his company "could possibly use a couple of million dollars cash to take advantage of some other opportunities." (I was not sophisticated enough at the time to realize that casual statements like this usually mean that the builder is in desperate financial straits.) He said he owned a large apartment development in St. Louis and that he might be interested in selling it outright rather than obtaining a second mortgage. He indicated, however, that it would take a total purchase price in the area of $10 million for him to have any serious interest in selling. (Again, I was too unsophisticated to realize that no matter how convincing a prospective seller is about the fact that he won't sell his property for less than a certain price, he is usually either lying at the outset or will eventually weaken and lower his price when a serious buyer enters the picture.)

As he talked, I roughly figured to myself that if I were successful in concluding such a sale I would earn a commission somewhere in the area of two to three hundred thousand dollars, based upon the Board of Realtors suggested commission scale. (Once more, I was not sophisticated enough to understand that sellers couldn't care less what a Board of Realtors thinks commissions should be.) I was excited over the fact that this was my first opportunity to get a shot at earning some big money. I tried hard to restrain my excitement so it wouldn't be too noticeable.

I told this Type Number Two professor that I felt

confident I could find a buyer for his St. Louis development if he would furnish me with all of the necessary information. I gave him a long list of items I thought I'd need in order to make a proper presentation, and he agreed to have his staff compile the data and get it to me within a week or so. All I needed now was a little something in writing and I'd be all set to shoot for the pot of gold at the end of the rainbow.

Unfortunately, I was so intimidated—so in awe of his "stature"—that I was very meek when I requested that we put into writing some kind of understanding as to my commission. When he finished lecturing me—emphasizing his reputation for "honesty" and "integrity" throughout the industry—I felt almost ashamed that I had insulted him by asking that he sign an agreement. Didn't I realize that when you deal with "honorable" men you don't need anything in writing? How dare I insult his "integrity." He was clearly the intimidator and I was clearly the intimidatee.

I backed off gracefully, assuring him that asking for an agreement was only a formality and that I was not worried about having anything in writing in his case. I then went back to my office and began laying out a game plan to market my first big deal. After I received all of the facts and figures from my Type Number Two professor's office, I made arrangements to fly to St. Louis to personally inspect the property. There was big money involved, and I was determined to do such a first class job in handling this deal that the seller would actually feel good about paying me a big commission (as you might suspect, I blush as I write this).

I sent letters to many of the biggest real estate buyers in the country, briefly describing the property and asking if they had any interest in the possible purchase of an apartment development of this size. I then sent a detailed presentation to those prospects who answered affirmatively; after a week or so I followed up the mailing of the presentations with phone calls.

One particular company indicated a very serious interest, and several phone calls and letters went back and forth between a certain gentleman at that company and me. (From here on I'll refer to that gentleman as the "buyer" even though he was actually only an employee of the company—the property acquisition man for a large real estate firm.)

I then made my second critical mistake (the first one, of course, was that I had let the seller convince me that I had no need for a signed commission agreement): instead of registering this buyer by certified mail, I merely began relaying offers and counter-offers between him and the seller by telephone (but I didn't mention the name of the buyer to the seller).

Then it happened: my professor began to smell the chips on the table and reared his ugly Type Number Two head. He told me he had just returned from New York where he had met a man who, by coincidence, turned out to be the buyer with whom I had been negotiating. He said another gentleman

had introduced him to the buyer, and that the buyer
had informed him that he'd been negotiating
through me for the purchase of his St. Louis apartment development.

As only a true Type Number Two can do, the
seller made it clear that he felt no obligation to me
regarding a possible sale to the buyer to whom I had
submitted his property. "Honesty" and "integrity"
were no longer the keynotes of his dissertations to
me. In true Type Number Two fashion, when the
time was ripe he had dropped his phony, flowery
talk and let me know, in no uncertain terms, that I
had better not reach for my chips.

I was shocked, demoralized and confused. I felt
as though someone had just kicked me in the kid-
neys. I tried to pull myself together and take a firm
stand, but the tougher I got, the nastier the seller
became. Finally, I committed the salesman's unfor-
giveable sin: I began to press. That brought it to a
head; we got into a near violent argument (he was a
"screamer"), and he "justified" his position by saying that I had contacted a great number of prospective buyers and that "anybody could do that." Although it was clear that I had been responsible for
calling the buyer's attention to the property and motivating his interest in it, I was dealing from a position of weakness. I had no commission agreement
with the seller; I had no certified letters showing that
I had registered the buyer with the seller; all I had
were what the seller had originally indicated to me
would be all that I would ever need: his "honesty"
and "integrity."

The kidding around was over so I fell back on my ace-in-the-hole—the one that had landed me the first $6,500 I had earned in the real estate business —and called my attorney into the picture. Once again it worked to the extent that the seller's attorney abided by the unwritten Universal Attorney-to-Attorney Respect Law and treated my attorney courteously; but it didn't get me the $200,000+ commission I felt I had earned.

When my attorney stepped in, the seller and his lawyer laid their whole hand on the table. They pointed out the third and most critical mistake I had made: not only did I not have a signed commission agreement or certified mail going for me, but I was missing the most important legal tool of all: a real estate salesman's license in the state of Missouri —the state where the property was located.

The seller's attorney proudly informed us that Missouri—like most other states—had a law on the books which prohibited unlicensed persons from working on the sale of properties located within the state. In the event of a sale, a seller had no legal obligation to pay a commission to anyone who did not have a real estate license in that state, even if the salesman were licensed in another state. My attorney quickly checked it out and confirmed that the seller's attorney had been absolutely correct.

Based on the circumstances—and considering the methods employed by my Type Number Two professor—I've always believed that I would not have received any commission at all had I not finally called my attorney into the picture. However, because of the unwritten Universal Attorney-to-Attorney Respect Law I ended up getting at least a pittance. Through his lawyer the seller told my attorney that if I kept my mouth shut and stayed completely out of the way, he would be generous and throw me a "bone" of $20,000. Talk about a position of weakness, that was a classic case. It was either a bone or nothing; I chose to take the bone.

My Type Number Two professor at Screw U. had taught me well. I had made one of the bigger real estate sales in the history of St. Louis and had walked away, not with the boxcar-sized commission I was entitled to, but with a merciful token amounting to about one-fourth of one percent of the selling price of the property. In the very first big deal I had ever worked on, I was missing not one, not two, but all three of the legal tools necessary for a real estate salesman to protect himself.

But because my professor had been so perfect an example, I felt that in the future I would be good at spotting Type Number Twos early. For one thing, I decided that whenever a man spent a great deal of time expounding on the virtues of "honesty" and "integrity," I would immediately be on guard and, preferably, avoid dealing with him at all. Secondly, I adopted the general standard that whenever a man refused to sign a commission agreement with me— regardless of the reason—I would automatically assume that he was a Type Number Two. (And I might point out that the future proved I had learned my lessons well.)

As with the Court Holder many years before, I thank you, also, Type Number Two professor . . . wherever you may be.

Chapter 8

My Senior Year At Screw U.

Translation: *The last of those early years of
learning through experience.*

As I said in the previous chapter, I always think of
the St. Louis fiasco as the single biggest turning
point in my career. More than any other deal I was
ever involved in, that situation forced me to clearly
face reality—the reality that the game of business is
played in a jungle and not on a playground; the reality that there are only three types of people in the
business world, and that all three were out to get my
chips; the reality that I had been dealing from a position of weakness. I vowed that I would find a way
to change my position to one of strength and that I
would begin to earn, and receive, big income. But I

didn't know exactly how I was going to go about it; after the St. Louis lesson I needed time to clear my head in order to formulate a workable game plan.

As it turned out, it took a little over a year to reach the point where I was able, with confidence, to put the finishing touches on such a game plan and be prepared to implement it. While the lessons of the St. Louis experience were fermenting in my mind, along with those learned from my Type Number One and Type Number Three professors, I still needed more practice in learning how to deal with the frustrations and humiliations of the jungle before I'd be mentally prepared to go after the big money. There was no way that I could have a positive attitude about accomplishing my objective unless I was completely prepared. The experiences of the next year or so—my remaining days at Screw U.—gave me that final necessary preparation.

In this chapter I relate three of those last experiences which most clearly stand out in my mind. All three had to do with second mortgage deals, and all three not only hammered home to me the fact that I was dealing from a position of weakness, but, just as importantly, made me realize—in conjunction with my St. Louis experience—that it was utterly absurd for me to work on small deals.

Following are brief accounts of those final three major "credits" that I needed to graduate from Screw U.:

Credit No. 1: Even though I had received $20,000 for selling the St. Louis property, I was still in very tight shape financially. My posture was not right because I needed every commission too badly. As you know, this is a very difficult thing for a person to hide. Even if you learn to masterfully disguise your words, the tone of your voice and your facial expressions will still give you away. The guy who is supposed to pay you a fee can sense your anxiety; you need the money, and he knows it. Such was the atmosphere at one of the second mortgage closings which took place shortly after the St. Louis sale.

My elderly friend—the Type Number One professor—had rejected this particular second mortgage proposal, so I had taken it to another lender. The one thing that stands out in my mind about this deal is that I probably worked harder on it than I did on my Kansas City closings less than two years later, yet I was paid—very begrudgingly—a fee of only $1,250 for my services (as opposed to fees in excess of $400,000 for my later, less tormenting work in selling the Kansas City properties). The controlling factor, of course, was that I needed that $1,250 badly at the time, and I let it show; I allowed myself to be intimidated. Think of it: the difference in these two examples—the difference between being intimidated and not being intimidated —was more than $400,000! That places quite a value on intimidation.

I can clearly remember the builder's attorney telling me at the closing, in so many words, that if I was a good boy and kept my mouth shut, I *might* get the $1,250 that was coming to me. As I sat there, humiliated, I asked myself what the hell I was even doing in that kind of situation to begin with. Why was I groveling around on my hands and knees like a beggar waiting to be thrown a few crumbs?

Finally, after many seemingly sadistic attempts on the part of the seller's attorney to worry me, the $1,250 bone was relinquished. If tortoises could bark, the attorney probably would have made me stand on my haunches and do so before tossing me the bone. From the standpoint of degradation that was the lowest point of my career at Screw U. It was a good experience, though, because as I sat through that closing—humbly doing whatever I was told to do, when I was told to do it—I vowed to rectify my posture so that I would not have to suffer through such degradation in the future. I made up my mind that I would find a way, first of all, to operate from a position of strength—to become unintimidatable —and, secondly, to work only on deals that had the potential of a payoff big enough to make my time and effort worthwhile.

Credit No. 2: This was another second mortgage deal that my Type Number One professor had turned down, so I had submitted it to another company. It was getting near graduation time at Screw U., and I was just about fed up with situations where I worked my tail off and then had to beg for a lousy bone. I had made up my mind that I was going to go for a substantial fee on this loan, though I realized I'd have to structure it in such a way that the borrower would not feel as though it were coming out of "his" money (shades of my first real estate deal in Cincinnati). It was a rather big loan request

"Down boy, down. Be good and keep your mouth shut, and I *might* throw it to you."

as second mortgages go—$500,000—but I felt the collateral was sound enough to support such a loan; the lender seemed to agree and expressed a serious interest in the deal.

After he sent his representative to inspect the property, I flew to New York to meet with the lender personally and see if there was anything I could do to help expedite a closing. At the meeting, I explained that I had quoted the prospective borrower an interest rate in the area of 13% plus a front end "discount" of 10%. I informed the lender that I had also told the prospective borrower that he (the lender) would be responsible for paying my fee. I reasoned that if the borrower paid me directly, he would never go along with my getting a $15,000 fee. On the other hand, if it were "tacked on"— much the same as in the Cincinnati deal—he'd think of it as coming out of the lender's money rather than out of "his" money. It was strictly psychological, but I had already learned that it was a necessary maneuver in dealing with most principals.

I explained to the lender that he needed only a 7% discount in order to bring his "effective" interest rate up to the normal back-breaking levels he was used to getting, and that he could therefore pay the additional 3% discount to me as my $15,000 fee.

The lender went crazy. During the ensuing heated discussion he said two things that would ring in my ears for a long time to come and, consequently, help to prepare me for earning, and receiving, substantial money in the near future.

The first thing he said was: "You have a lot of nerve trying to earn $15,000 on one deal; why, you're only a broker."

Boy, did that ever make me see the light. My posture was all wrong; I was *only* a broker. I had no "right" to earn $15,000 on one deal. It was all right for the lender to earn that much—and more—for such "services" and "privileges" as "prepaid interest," "discount fees" and "prepayment penalties." It was all right for the lender simply because he had the right posture; he was dealing from a position of strength. People don't generally begrudge a wealthy man making money, but I was trying to violate an unwritten rule of business—the rule that a poor guy doesn't have the "right" to make money.

His second remark, however, was even more unbelievable: the lender said that it was "unconscionable" for me to be charging a 3% brokerage fee for the placement of a second mortgage loan.

By that time I was at the point where I had to restrain myself from laughing out loud. It actually sounded humorous when he said it because—knowing the facts as I did—I wondered how he could make such a statement in a serious vein. Be that as it may, he did speak those words with a straight face and he definitely was serious. Here was a man who had built his fortune on the misfortune and financial desperation of others, who earned interest rates of 15% and more by using hidden charge gimmicks such as "prepaid interest," "discount fees" and "prepayment penalties," and who was now saying

"You have a lot of nerve trying to earn $15,000 on one deal;
why, you're only a broker."

that it was "unconscionable" for *me* to make $15,000 on one deal.

Among other things, the Theory of Relativity was illustrated in this situation. Relative to the kind of profits the lender was used to making, my fee was insignificant. But relative to what brokers were used to having to settle for, it was "unconscionable." It was obvious that the only way a person could ever hope to get his "relativity status" upgraded was to find a method for changing his posture in such a way that he would be thought of as one of those people who had the "right" to earn big money.

Needless to say, the deal never closed. It did not close because I had "stepped out of line" by trying to earn what I considered at the time to be big money, without being prepared to pull it off. But with my lessons at Screw U. nearly fermented in my mind, I was just about ready to make such preparations—preparations for elevating my posture to a level where I could no longer be intimidated—and thus graduate from Screw U.

Credit No. 3: This was the final course—the one that tied the ribbon around my diploma. It was a second mortgage loan on an apartment development in Tampa. My Type Number One professor had turned down the loan application, so once again I had taken the deal to another second mortgage lender and was able to generate some serious interest.

Having fulfilled most of my educational requirements at Screw U., I was savvy enough to be able to spot—almost from the outset—the warning signs which indicated that I was going to have considerable trouble collecting my fee if a deal were closed. I was now educated enough to have been successful in getting the borrower to sign a commission agreement with me, and of course I didn't need a real estate license in the state of Florida because this deal did not involve the sale of a property. I was again shooting for an "unconscionable" fee of $15,000, only this time it was even more "unconscionable" because it was based on a much smaller loan than the previous one had been. And this time my fee wasn't buried in with the lender's front end "discount;" I was to receive it directly from the borrower.

As things progressed and it began to look like the deal was going to be made, I became so certain that the borrower had no intention of paying me my $15,000 fee that I devised a specific plan to try to protect myself. I decided I would not give the borrower any indication that I intended to be present at the closing. I knew it would never occur to him that a loan broker would fly halfway across the country to collect a fee at a closing, simply because it was unheard-of for any broker to do so. Normally (and mistakenly) a broker just waits for his commission check to be sent to him in the mail. (If you ever ventured into a loan broker's office and were surprised to see a cobweb-covered skeleton—cigar butt between its teeth—sitting behind the desk, you probably stumbled onto a broker who was waiting for his commission check to be mailed to him.)

I figured as long as it didn't occur to the borrow-

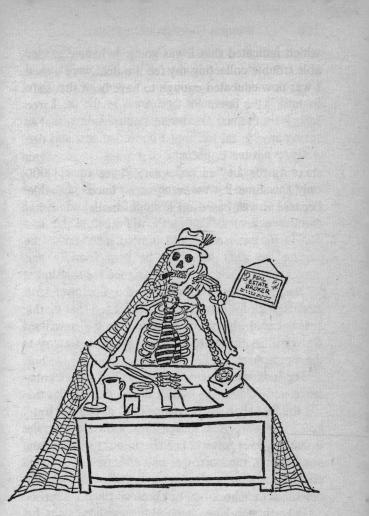

"Miss Jones, has the commission check arrived yet?"

er that I might attend the closing, he would not go to the trouble, in advance, of taking proper measures to maneuver me out of the way as my Type Number Two professor had done in the St. Louis deal. I didn't even discuss my commission with him during any of our telephone conversations, and certainly he never mentioned it to me.

As it turned out, I had a very important appointment scheduled for the same day as the Tampa closing, so I sent my assistant (whom I had hired several months earlier) to Tampa the night before the loan was to be finalized. I told him to show up at the closing the next morning, be very friendly and matter-of-fact, and present my signed fee agreement to the attorneys representing the borrower and lender. With his legal background, I felt that my assistant could also serve to introduce the unwritten Universal Attorney-toAttorney Respect Law into the atmosphere.

The next evening my assistant called me long distance and related the events of the closing, including the fact that the borrower had, to say the least, been very surprised to see him walk through the door. However, after a certain amount of stuttering and stalling, the borrower had endorsed a $15,000 check in my name. But what horrified me was the news that the check had not been certified.

Even though I had been almost without sleep for several days prior to this and was exhausted from having worked without a break since early that morning, my wheels started turning a mile a minute when he told me that the check wasn't certified; I had learned long before that an uncertified check could be the same as no check at all. I quickly called the airlines and found that if I really hurried I had just enough time to throw a few things in a bag and make it to the airport for a late evening flight to Tampa. On top of everything else, I hadn't eaten a thing all day and I was ravenous. My mental scales instantly weighed the two sides: on the one side were my hunger and exhaustion, as well as the horrible thought of traveling all the way to Tampa late at night; on the other side was $15,000. The $15,000 won out. I grabbed a few necessities, made sure that I had sufficient money and identification, stuffed a handful of crackers in my mouth, and jumped in the car.

As is always the case with late evening flights, the trip was miserable. I arrived in Tampa feeling like a corpse. My assistant met me at the airport, and we then hurried to the motel where he was staying; I quickly checked into a room, and we sat down to discuss the strategy.

As The Tortoise, I had always counted on the other guy making the mistake of pausing at some point. Maybe he had a drink first, or ate lunch, or got some other work done, or put "it" off until tomorrow because it was too late in the day, but I always counted on my opponent getting just a little bit lax so that the Tortoise and Hare Theory could take effect ("If you slow down enough to look over your right shoulder, I'll pass you on the left; if you slow down enough to look over your left shoulder, I'll pass you on the right.") I had traveled halfway across the country based on an assumption and a gamble: the assumption was that the borrower was going to stop payment on the $15,000 check; the gamble was that he would be just lax enough not to take care of the matter as soon as the bank opened in the morning.

I grabbed a couple hours of restless sleep and rolled out of the sack much earlier than necessary; I was taking no chances on not being at the front door of the bank when it opened. I felt like death warmed over, but a cold shower and the thought of $15,000 stimulated me enough to keep moving. So there I was—black business suit, black-rimmed sunglasses and black briefcase—standing in front of the bank, waiting for it to open.

Needless to say, I was the first customer through the door that day. I walked directly over to a teller window and presented the $15,000 check for payment. Laying out all of my identification cards, I said that I'd like the $15,000 in cash, with as many large bills as possible so that it would fit in my briefcase. Well, let me tell you something: you haven't lived until you've walked into a strange bank, in a strange town—wearing a black suit, black-rimmed sunglasses, and carrying a black briefcase—and tried to cash a $15,000 check. I think everyone in the bank assumed that whatever it was I was up to, it had to be illegal. Within minutes, a whole army of bank employees was buzzing around trying to help figure out what to do about this unheard-of request: someone—a strange someone at that—was actually demanding that a bank come up with real live cash in place of a check.

A bank officer finally took charge and said that he would have to call the person who had endorsed the check to make certain it was not a forged endorsement. (Actually the check had been disbursed on an attorney's trust account directly to the borrower, and the borrower had then endorsed it in my name.) I argued that the check was drawn on his bank, that he could see the attorney's signature on the front of the check was a valid one, and that he was able to confirm that the funds were in the account, so there was no reason to call the endorser. (I knew that a call to the borrower/endorser would be an open invitation to a dispute that would probably result, one way or another, in payment being stopped on the check.) Nevertheless the bank officer persisted.

My wheels started turning again, faster this time. I quickly thought to myself that even if the borrower was intending to try to somehow stop payment on the check, he probably had not had time to think through just how he was going to do it. After all, he had been taken by surprise when my assistant showed up at the closing. I was counting on the fact that he—like a true hare—would "figure it out tomorrow." I thought there was a good chance that the attorney who had disbursed the money for the lender might not yet know what the borrower's intention was (again, I'm assuming that the borrower's intention was, in fact, to stop payment).

After thinking it through, I told him it was my

understanding that the endorser of the check (borrower) was out of town that day. I suggested that he instead call the attorney who had signed the check, since he was a customer of the bank anyway. I was in luck. The bank officer called the attorney, and, although he was surprised to hear that I was not only in town, but at the bank trying to cash the $15,000 check, he confirmed the fact that he had signed the check and watched the borrower endorse it in my name.

Then came a scene right out of a movie:

There I was, standing in front of the teller's cage in my black suit and black-rimmed sunglasses, stuffing $15,000 cash into a black briefcase as a security guard stood by. It was not until I clicked my bulging briefcase closed and noticed that everyone in the bank was staring that it occurred to me what the scene must look like. There's a saying about "crying all the way to the bank;" I won't comment on that one, but I will tell you this: I *laughed* all the way *from* the bank.

I have no way of knowing if it ever came to pass, but the thought that the borrower might have been calling the bank or the attorney to see if there was a way he could stop payment on the check—while I was on my way to the airport carrying a briefcase filled with $15,000 in cash—made the nightmare of the previous twelve hours all worthwhile.

On the plane trip home, as I lay back in my seat —thoroughly exhausted—I told myself that the time had arrived. No more crawling around on my hands and knees and no more penny ante deals;

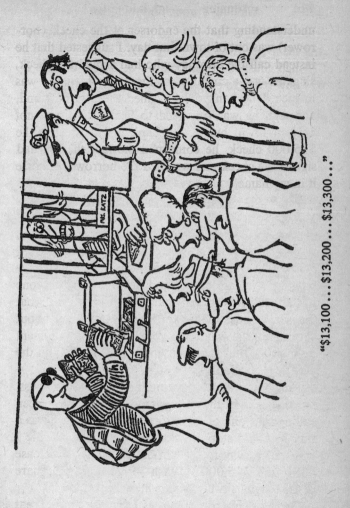

"$13,100 . . . $13,200 . . . $13,300 . . ."

from now on I was going to have the right posture
and the money was going to be big.

I had finished my education at Screw U. and I
was now ready to prepare myself for graduation.

Chapter 9

My Graduation From Screw U.

Translation: *Organizing my philosophy and making preparations for applying it.*

After completing my Tampa "credit," there was no question in my mind that I was ready to graduate from Screw U. The time had come to organize into usable form the philosophy I had been developing, and to lay out specific techniques for applying it. Once that was done I knew I would then be prepared to attempt to accomplish my financial objective.

I explained my plans to my assistant, but to my surprise he wasn't enthusiastic. I asked him what was causing his lack of enthusiasm, and his reply dumbfounded me. (In view of later events, it seems even more incredible to me now than it did then.) He said it just didn't seem "right" to him that I was planning to suddenly change my whole operation from small second mortgage loans to large property sales. His "reasoning" was that I had not yet really "succeeded" (by some strange standard he was using) in the second mortgage business, yet here I was switching my efforts to another area of real estate just when I was starting to do well. He said he felt guilty about it (society had done a good job of brainwashing him), although he couldn't explain exactly why. From the sound of his remarks it seemed almost as though he thought I had some sort of mysterious "moral" obligation (moral by whose standards?—remember the Theory of Relativity?)—to the people in the real estate industry, society, or some other abstract entity—to keep my nose to the grindstone, work hard, and come up through the ranks "one step at a time," letting progress take its "natural" course.

The whole idea seemed so repulsive that, after giving it considerable thought, my subconscious mind rebelled and inspired me to formulate a new theory. I appropriately named it the

LEAPFROG THEORY

The best way to explain the Leapfrog Theory is to simply point out that it says exactly the opposite of what my assistant was trying to say. The Leapfrog Theory states that a person has no legal or moral obligation or, for that matter, logical reason to "work his way up through the ranks." It says, in fact, that every person has the inherent right to "self-proclaim"—to announce, at any time he chooses, that he is on any level he chooses to be on.

The quickest way to the top is not by fighting your way *through* the pack; the quickest way is to leapfrog *over* the pack and simply take it upon yourself to proclaim that you're above it. Regardless of what anyone tells you, you do have the right to self-proclamation. There is a catch, however: if you are not prepared to be above it, then, in spite of the fact that you make such a proclamation, the realities of the business world will knock you right back into the pack in a very short period of time.

On the other hand, if you are prepared—as I was when I graduated from Screw U.—you then have a good chance of staying above the pack. The terrible waste occurs when you're prepared to be above it, but spend your valuable time and energy fighting your battles within the pack—battling your way up "through the ranks." When you're prepared, an understanding of the Leapfrog Theory can save you from having to endure years of unnecessary frustration. You proclaim yourself to be above others in your field, "leapfrog" over them, and eliminate your competition by simply refusing to acknowledge it. Without authority from anyone else—and without being saddled by mystical "guilt feelings" or "moral obligations"—you simply take it upon yourself to begin operating on a higher level. You don't wait for the industry, society, or some other abstract entity to christen you a "heavyweight" in your business.

(Had I listened to my assistant's "logic," I would probably still be crawling around on my hands and knees collecting "bones" begrudgingly thrown to me by unappreciative second mortgage borrowers. Instead, by acting on the Leapfrog Theory I was able to receive—less than five months later—a commission which was, by itself, approximately twice the *combined* total of all the commissions I had been paid during my first three years in the real estate business. To say, then, that the Leapfrog Theory proved to be sound would be the understatement of the century.)

Once I made the decision to go the leapfrog route, I committed myself to doing a lot of thinking and planning—to getting specific. I went over my most memorable experiences—both prior to and during my years at Screw U.—one by one, extracted the lessons I had learned and the theories I had developed, and worked on organizing them into usable form. I spent many afternoons away from my office—sitting on a big rock next to a river—just thinking and taking notes. After a while I began organizing my notes into logical order and found that they led me to intimidation as the very root of the problem of earning, and receiving, big money. I therefore decided that intimidation would be my first order of business; it would be the key to my usable philosophy.

Thinking back on my own experiences and observations over the years, I determined that the problems most people have in reaching their objectives revolve around the fact that they constantly allow themselves to be intimidated. In real estate this means being intimidated by the buyers and sellers of properties (or in the case of the second mortgage business, the lenders and borrowers); in a field such as insurance it means being intimidated by the prospect; and in life in general it means being intimidated by "the other guy," whoever he may be. The problem is always the same regardless of the situation. Stated in theory form, it becomes the

THEORY OF INTIMIDATION

Write this one on the inside of your shirt cuff because it's critical in determining the outcome of most situations. This theory states that the results a person obtains are inversely proportionate to the degree to which he is intimidated. (It was in the deals in which I had been the most intimidated that I had taken the greatest financial beatings; and it was in the situations in which I had been intimidated the least that I had made out the best.) It was clear, then, that the first step in organizing my philosophy into usable form was to lay out a specific plan to keep from being intimidated. I had to create a method for trading places with the principal; from now on I would have to be the intimidator and find a way to maneuver the principal into the role of the intimidatee.

At that point I had defined the problem and identified my objective (to reverse the roles of the principal and me). To find a way to solve the problem, however, I first had to analyze its causes. Why had I been the intimidatee in the first place? Using a very analytical approach, the answer I came up with was the fact that my posture had been all wrong. I knew I had more knowledge and ability than most of the principals I had been dealing with, and it seemed as though this should have been obvious when I spoke to them; but my knowledge and ability were not important so long as my posture remained weak. The fact that I had knowledge and ability was not relevant; what was relevant was the status of my posture at the time I spoke. Put into theory form, you have the

POSTURE THEORY

This theory states that it's not what you say or do that counts, but what your posture is when you say or do it. In real estate sales, for example, if your posture suggests that you're "only a broker" (remember the second mortgage lender who thought that my fee was "unconscionable?")—if the principals see you as nothing more than an unnecessary annoyance in their deal—then you're going to be intimidated no matter how great your knowledge and ability, and no matter what you say or do.

If intimidation was the problem and a weak posture was the cause, then what was the cure? How could I improve my weak posture? I had to figure out a way to maneuver myself into a position of power. And when I thought of power I remembered my old Type Number One professor who was the epitome of someone in an impermeable position; his posture was a picture of strength. He was powerful because he had wealth, which in turn gave him his image. I analyzed that his wealth gave him "real power," but that his image also gave him a certain "abstract power."

I then thought about several people whom I knew to be generally respected and/or feared, playing the game from a position of strength even though they were not wealthy. I realized that these people had something else going for them: image. I could no longer operate as "only a broker;" I had to have an image that would be awesome to the principals I worked with. They had to respect me so much that they would feel I—like wealthy people—had a "right" to earn big money. This was the easiest step for me to accomplish, and as you'll see in the next chapter I created a thorough technique for changing my image. (Because I do explain it in detail in the next chapter, I won't discuss it any further here. The important thing right now is just to point out that I did recognize the importance of "image power" with regard to my posture and that I therefore made plans to upgrade my image.)

As to real power, since I didn't have wealth behind me, I knew it would be harder to attain. I certainly didn't want to rely solely on abstract power— image—without having anything to back it up. In thinking it through I came to the conclusion that I had to be backed up by "legal power;" I reasoned that if I had the proper legal tools on my side, I would then have the real power I needed. During my years at Screw U. I had become more and more fanatical about having all of my "t's" crossed and "i's" dotted. Through experience I had also learned that whenever I brought my attorney into a situation, the unwritten Universal Attorney-to-Attorney Respect Law was injected into the atmosphere and usually worked to my advantage. I reasoned, however, that if both my legal power and image power were strong from the outset, then my posture would be so potent that my having an attorney represent me at closings would only be a formality—a sort of "frosting on the cake," as it were.

The key to legal power was for me to convert my own past experiences into the proper legal tools. I had certainly endured enough beatings at Screw U. to be able to recognize that there are basically three strong legal tools at the disposal of any real estate salesman who has the courage, ambition and persistence to use them.

The first tool was a real estate license. In the future I would have to be licensed in the state where the property was located. (Eventually, through the expenditure of considerable time, energy and money, I obtained twelve real estate licenses—eleven states plus the District of Columbia.)

The second legal tool was to obtain a signed commission agreement with the seller before beginning to work on his property. My experience had taught me that it was nothing short of suicide to work on a deal on the basis of only a verbal understanding—in *any* kind of business. Knowing this, I had been amazed to find—during my days at Screw U.—that most salesmen who work on the sale of large properties do not have written commission agreements with the sellers. I believed that this is due to a combination of intimidatability and the failure to face reality. Just as I had been intimidated by my Type Number Two professor, I think that most salesmen are repeatedly intimidated by sellers when it comes to trying to obtain written commission agreements. After being victimized time after time, the salesman still fails to face the reality that it is not in the seller's best interest to see him receive a big commission—or any commission at all, for that matter.

I had become fairly successful at having the courage and persistence to get signed commission agreements from borrowers and sellers, but "fairly successful" would no longer be good enough. I made up my mind that in the future—no matter how good the deal or how big its potential—I wouldn't even consider working on it unless the seller signed a commission agreement as the first step.

The third legal tool was certified mail. At Screw U. I had observed that whenever I used certified mail to submit a deal to a lender or buyer, or to register the name of a lender or buyer with a borrower or seller, the principals at least seemed to acknowledge the part I was playing in the deal. I reasoned that this was because they were aware of the fact that if a lawsuit ever developed over the payment of my commission, the introduction of certified slips and letters into court proceedings would be very conclusive. I had reached the point where I was using certified mail in most of my deals, but this would no longer be satisfactory. I laid out a plan for a system of certified mail communication that would be so intricate it would practically prove my case in court if I ever had to go to that extreme to collect a commission.

While these legal tools could be very important factors if I were ever forced to file suit, their primary purpose was to help me to *avoid* lawsuits; just as countries spend vast amounts on armaments—not to attack other countries but to defend themselves against attack—so it was that I looked upon the three legal tools as my "civil defense."

With the techniques I describe in the next chapter, I'd have abstract power; with the use of my three legal tools, I'd have real power; however, I wanted to go one step further: I wanted to back up both my abstract power and real power by actually being the best at what I did—"performance power." In being the best, I would not only have an impressive image and the real power of the proper legal tools on my side, but—by everyone's standards—I also would have performed satisfactorily. I would not just be impressive and I would not just have the seller by the throat legally; I would really "deserve" to be paid my commission. In other words, my image would not be a phony one and, if it became necessary, my legal tools would be backed up in court by the clear evidence that I had done my job well. I had always been very regimented in my work habits and had turned out extremely neat, detailed presentations, but in the future I would have to become a fanatic on operational procedures. I wanted to make it almost impossible for anyone to be able to say, with a straight face, that I had not done enough to earn my commission. From now on I would have to see to it that it was obvious to everyone involved that the progress and conclusion of the sale were due mainly to my efforts.

I would obtain my objective—a strong posture—through abstract power (image), real power (legal tools) and performance power (execution). The Theory of Intimidation and the Posture Theory capped off the philosophy I had been developing prior to—and primarily during—my undergraduate days at Screw U. And I felt I could apply this philosophy to any phase of life; the fact that I intended to use it to earn, and receive, big commissions in the real estate business was incidental.

The old, inefficient, "unworkable" building was now replaced by a new, efficient, and—I hoped—"workable" structure: my philosophy. The skeleton of that philosophy consisted of the theories I've described thus far, as well as other theories I'll be talking about in later chapters. The very bedrock under the entire structure was the Theory of Reality; every theory was either directly or indirectly related to the Theory of Reality, so the philosophy itself was really a philosophy of reality.

Now my philosophy had not only been developed, it was also organized. Everything was clearly in place in my mind. I had not just lived through the experiences, I had converted them into what I hoped would be a usable form—a *workable* philosophy.

All that was left to do was develop specific techniques for applying the philosophy to the particular phase of life that I was most concerned with at any given time. As I said, my foremost concern at that particular time happened to be the earning, and receiving, of big real estate commissions; therefore the techniques I devised for applying the philosophy were oriented accordingly. It is my firm belief, however, that the philosophy can just as easily be adapted to any other line of work; it is only the techniques that differ from one business to another.

I finally felt confident that I knew, in most instances, what was the right thing to do; however, I also knew it was more natural to do the instinctive thing in any given set of circumstances, even though instinctive action is wrong more often than not. In order to apply my philosophy, then, I would have to become unwavering in my determination to do the right thing, rather than be panicked into doing the instinctive thing.

I knew it wasn't going to be easy. I knew that once I made the self-proclamation of being "above the pack"—once I announced to the world that I had leapfrogged to a new level—the proverbial heat in the kitchen would be turned up considerably. Like every person who has ever had the guts to go after something better, I knew I would be the object of attack from many directions if I carried through with my plans; I knew I would be inviting jealousy and resentment. I also faced the reality, however, that jealousy, resentment, and increased heat are natural by-products of getting ahead.

After enduring what I had over the past several years, a little jealousy, resentment and heat seemed like a small price to pay in return for dignity, peace of mind, and money. Being liked was not much of a reward for being poor and disrespected; on the other hand, having money and being respected were more than enough consolation for having a few people dislike me.

In the next section of this book I divide selling into five basic steps. (If you don't happen to be a "salesman," that's irrelevant; the general principles—*not* the techniques—apply to every phase of life.) You might already be aware of the first four steps; in order to be "successful" in selling, you must:

1) Obtain a product to sell (e.g., a woman's "product" could very well be *herself* —as a wife),

2) Locate a market for the product (in the above example this would consist of available men who meet her standards),

3) Implement a marketing method (put into effect a procedure for selling herself), and

4) Be able to close the sale (get the stiff to sign on the dotted line and hand over the ring).

I've seen these four steps discussed in many sales books, but interestingly enough I've never seen the fifth—and by far the most important—step discussed in *any* book. That seems incomprehensible to me, but because it is so, I took the liberty to name it myself. I call it the "Bottom Line Step;" you must:

5) GET PAID!

In this entire book, the above two words are the only ones I've underlined. That should give you some idea as to where I place "getting paid" in order of importance. If you recall, throughout this book I've used such expressions as "earning, and *receiving*, big commissions" and "earning, and *receiving*, income;" earning is one thing, but *receiving* is something else altogether. (After the gal closes the deal—gets the signature and the hardware from her "prospect"—she still has to get paid; she must do those things necessary for receiving the goodies available from a successful marriage.)

In the next section you'll also see the specific *techniques* I used in applying my philosophy to the five steps of selling as they pertain to real estate. It will become obvious to you that all of the techniques I used in the first four steps were oriented toward successfully completing the final and most important step: *getting paid*.

(Before getting into Section III—wherein I describe the specific techniques I used in applying my philosophy to the earning, and receiving, of jumbo-sized real estate commissions—let me first emphasize that these techniques were not only developed specifically for real estate selling, but for a specialized area of real estate selling: the sale of large income-producing properties. In addition, the techniques were specifically tailored to fit my own personality and objectives.

(Therefore, it doesn't necessarily follow that the exact same techniques will work for the selling of insurance or even for the selling, say, of single residence homes. Further, techniques must also vary according to someone's goals and type of personality.

(*It's the philosophy itself that holds the basic truisms, that contains the realities applicable not only from one business to another, but to all phases of life.* The trick is to understand your own personality and objectives, as well as the specific peculiarities of your own business or area of interest, and then to develop precise techniques for applying the realities of the philosophy to them.

(As I stated, my techniques for applying the philosophy to the selling of real estate were all directly or indirectly geared to trying to make certain that I got paid if I were successful in effecting a sale. Food for thought: in your particular area of interest, be it business, love, or life in general, what accomplishment would you classify as the Bottom Line Step—"getting paid?")

It had been a long road I'd traveled, a road often lined with frustration, humiliation and confusion, and with experiences which would have tested the patience of Job. But The Tortoise, not knowing any better, had just kept trudging ahead. Now he was finally prepared; he was ready to graduate from Screw U. and begin playing the game for big chips.

The philosophy I had developed was a direct result of recognizing and acknowledging the brutal realities I had encountered in the jungle. If my philosophy proved to be workable—as I felt confident it would—it should then result in my earning, and receiving, sizable real estate commissions.

As I stood at the gates of Screw U. for the last time, I looked back at my three stereotype professors who were observing my departure. With arms spread and raised above my head—each hand motioning a victory sign—I smiled warmly and said, "Let me make one thing perfectly clear: you won't have Robert Ringer to kick around anymore."

With that I turned and made my final exit through the gates, humming the Screw U. alma mater as I walked away.

"Let me make one thing perfectly clear: You won't have Robert Ringer to kick around anymore."

THE TECHNIQUES I USED TO WIN

Translation: How I Applied My Philosophy To My Specific Objective.

Chapter 10

Using Posture Power
To Get The Ball

Translation: *Obtaining a product to sell.*

My first rule in obtaining a product to sell was to avoid working with other salesmen—or as they say in the trade: "co-brokering." My experience had taught me that the worst possible way to obtain a deal was to try to get it from another salesman. Yet I had observed that co-brokering was a way of life for many people in the business. Rather than spend the time, energy and money necessary to solicit listings directly from principals, many salesmen take the easy way out and just work on deals passed along by others. A salesman who operates this way is seldom, if ever, involved in the closing of a sale, and when one of the deals he "works on" does happen to close, he's so far removed from the man who is supposed to pay the commission that it's a minor miracle if he ever receives a dime for his nominal efforts. He is skirting the real battlefield where it all takes place: the direct confrontation with the Type Number One, Two or Three who must eventually be reckoned with in every sale.

I've known many salesmen who spend day after day discussing multi-million dollar deals with other salesmen, apparently deriving their thrills from the conversation alone. They steer clear of the excruciating effort necessary just to secure a listing directly from a serious seller, let alone the effort it takes to locate a market for the property, implement a marketing method and close the sale. This type of salesman limits his efforts to recopying (as cheaply as possible) sheets of already blurred and scanty information regarding the property, then passes these dingy looking reproductions on to other salesmen. His hope is that one of the other salesmen will somehow get lucky and sell the property, and then—the ultimate hope—a small piece of the commission (if there is one) will miraculously find its way back to him.

I'm not saying that a real estate salesman should never work with another salesman under any circumstance; that would be ideal, but it's not always practical. (Circumstances regarding two of the sales I discuss in the last section of this book were such that it made sense for me to pay a fee to another broker. Even in those two cases, however, I took matters into my own hands and tried to control the flow of information and destiny of the sale.) What I *am* saying is that co-brokering should be avoided whenever possible, and that co-brokering as a regular habit is the best way I know of to increase the odds against receiving commissions.

In *any* type of pursuit in life, you are "co-brokering" if you avoid the arena—the place where it's all happening—choosing instead to "work" with your counterparts.

In simplest terms: the shortest distance between two points is a straight line; when you "co-broker," you form a triangle. The odds against closing a big deal—in any type of business—are staggering, even when you're working directly with "principals;" to try to do it with a third party between you and the person or persons who are in a position to say "yes" or "no" is almost masochistic.

Working primarily on apartment developments, the smallest project I was initially interested in was 100 units; later I increased my minimum to 200 units but didn't really get excited over any deal that was much under 300.

The first step was to determine if an owner had any interest in selling his property. When I phoned an owner I came right out and introduced myself before even being asked who I was. In a very matter-of-fact tone I would tell his secretary that I wanted to talk to the owner about a personal matter. If his secretary insisted on knowing the nature of my call, I then told her that it regarded the pur-

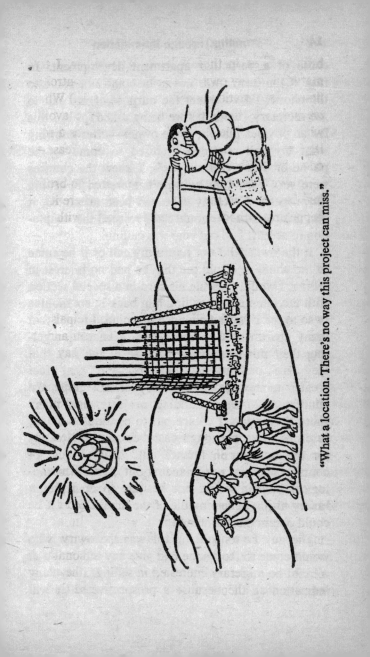

"What a location. There's no way this project can miss."

chase of a particular apartment development. In fact, if the owner was not in or could not come to the phone, I'd volunteer the purpose of my call to the secretary (again before being asked). I did this for an obvious reason: if the owner—after knowing what my call regarded—refused to come to the phone or didn't call me back, I knew the chances were very good that he wasn't interested in selling his property. Certainly if he had been interested, it was unlikely that he could have resisted the temptation to at least find out who was calling.

If the owner did not return my call or if he came to the phone and told me that he had no interest in selling, I would then file his card in a special section with the intention of calling him back in six months or so to see if he had changed his mind. I found that many apartment developers have a knack for getting their minds changed because of the fact that they are pathological builders—and that fact creates money problems. They cannot resist the temptation to keep building projects, and many times they have no choice but to continue building in order to keep enough cash "circulating" to pay for the last "I can finance out" deal (which, of course, ended up *not* financing out). A true pathological builder would not hesitate to construct a luxury hi-rise in the middle of the Sinai Desert if he could obtain the financing for it.

The guy I was looking for was the owner who would come to the phone and give any indication at all that he might be interested in selling. I say "any indication at all" because a prospective seller will rarely, if ever, come right out and say that he definitely wants to sell his property. My experience had taught me that even if a man were desperately trying to sell his property, he would still be very casual when talking to a person about it for the first time. I became sophisticated enough to realize that when an owner gave me the old line of, "I've never given it any thought, but I'm always willing to listen to offers," he was, in fact, really a serious seller.

Builder-owners, bless their hearts, are a strange lot. Not only do they not necessarily mean what they say, but most of the time they don't even mean what they think they mean. They live in a whole different world—one that revolves around "the next deal"— and they speak a completely different language. What I did was learn to translate that language into simple English. For example, "I'm always willing to listen" often means: "I'm desperate."

If the owner did display an interest in selling, my next step was to obtain some basic figures about his property in order to determine whether or not the deal was makable. I did not ask the owner for these facts during the same conversation, however, because I had not yet established my posture with him. Screw U. had taught me that one of the first things a seller does to firmly establish his position as the intimidator is to make the salesman justify his very reason for existing. Once the seller threw that blunt "Who are you?" at me, my posture would be ruined because no matter how I responded I would probably still come across as "just another real estate broker"—and an owner needs another real estate broker about as much as he needs another vacant apartment.

So my technique was geared to establishing image power in an effort to avoid having to justify myself. As per the Leapfrog Theory, I not only had to be above being "just another broker," but I had to be beyond even being asked who I was. I had to be so far removed from the rest of the pack that the owner would be too intimidated to ask such a question.

I solved this problem by having a special "calling card" designed. The calling card was specifically created to accomplish two objectives: the first, as I already pointed out, was to eliminate the question of who I was; the second was to make it almost impossible for an owner to forget me, so that if and when he ever decided to sell his property, the chances were good that he'd contact The Tortoise.

The calling card that accomplished both of these objectives was a spectacular brochure costing nearly $5 a copy. The dimensions of this calling card were roughly 10" x 10", and it had a hard cover like a published book. The cover itself was pitch-black—with a high-gloss finish—and it opened from bottom to top rather than right to left like most books. Centered on that glossy black front cover was a breathtaking full-color photo of the earth as seen from an Apollo spaceship. Not only was my name not displayed on the front cover, but it did not even appear on the inside of the cover or on the first page.

In fact the only thing that appeared on the inside front cover were the words:

"Earth
To Life .... Support
To the Explorer .. A Base
To the Wise ..... An Investment"

On the first page following the inside cover appeared a round picture of a telescopic view looking down on metropolitan Chicago. By the time I finally got around to mentioning my name on the next page, there was not much that need be said. Obviously, anyone who used a spectacular $5 brochure as his calling card must be *somebody*. Obviously, anyone who didn't feel that it was necessary even to mention his name on the front cover or first two pages of the brochure must be *somebody*.

The remainder of the brochure consisted primarily of brief statements alluding to my general expertise in the field of real estate. It also contained an abundance of dramatic pictures, logos, maps and other carefully selected items that made it "obvious" who I was.

In short, the brochure was intimidating.

It wasn't that anyone understood what I did for a living after reading the brochure, but only that they knew I was not just another member of the pack— not "just another real estate broker." I was obviously "somebody;" I was beyond justifying my existence. Rarely did anyone ask me to explain anything more about myself after receiving the "Earth brochure." Furthermore, because of its spectacular nature the recipient of the brochure found it almost impossible to throw it away. Many people kept it right on their desks—as a conversation piece—or, at the very least, somewhere close by where they could point it out to visitors.

Thus, ideally, before the owner of a property asked me to explain who I was, I took the initiative and suggested that I send him some information about myself before getting into any of the details regarding his property. Once again this was a technique that separated me from the rest of the pack because it was the antithesis of how a real estate salesman normally talks to an owner. Now it was The Tortoise who was being casual, as though no one deal were that important; it was The Tortoise who was suggesting that the owner learn something about him before proceeding further, rather than stuttering and stammering in an effort to justify his very existence to the owner.

After mailing the Earth brochure to the owner, I would usually wait a week or so before calling him back. And when I did I normally got through to him right away. After the unusual nature of my initial telephone inquiry, followed by the arrival of my spectacular "calling card," the casting of the roles was beginning to take shape. I was positioning myself to become the intimidator, while giving the owner the opportunity, for the first time, to try out for the part of the intimidatee. I was developing abstract strength in the form of an impressive image; my posture was correct from the start.

Now I was in a position to further qualify the

property by having the owner tell me the most pertinent facts over the phone. I developed a set formula for calculating, in a matter of seconds, whether or not there was at least a remote chance that the deal was makable.

The point is that I was not just interested in knowing whether or not the owner wanted to sell his property; I also wanted to know whether or not it was *salable*. Earlier in this book I gave the opinion that the number one cause of failure in any field of endeavor is the inability to recognize and/or refusal to acknowledge reality; then at the beginning of this chapter I pointed out one of the more important realities—that co-brokering is, by and large, a waste of time; and yet another important reality when it comes to working on the sale of large properties (or, for that matter, the sale of *anything* large —regardless of the industry) is the fact that the majority of deals simply are not makable (meaning that the properties, for any one of a number of reasons, are not salable).

Therefore, as I became more and more experienced, I also became more and more selective as to the properties I worked on.

As I've said so many times, the chances of closing any major deal—regardless of how good it is—are very slim to begin with. But if it's not a good deal, the odds against a closing become almost infinite. Because of this, part of my technique was to implement the

MAKABLE DEAL THEORY

This theory points out the efficiency of expending your efforts in working hard to find a few makable deals, rather than working hard on an endless number of unmakable deals and clinging to the faint hope that you'll somehow close one. I concentrated on finding that one good deal, rather than working on thirty bad ones and adhering to the prayer that luck and the law of averages would eventually bring about a positive result.

I cannot emphasize enough what an important step this was for me. I noted that many people have a masochistic tendency to work on "pie-in-the-sky" deals—deals that have almost no possibility of ever closing. In real estate, it's like drug addiction, with the owner being the doper and the salesman the dopee: with tremendous consistency, owners seem to have salesmen hooked on the fantasy that unmakable deals can somehow be made.

What I discovered was that the makability of a deal revolved primarily around "cash flow" (the cash that is left over after deduction of all expenses and mortgage payments from the income), also commonly referred to as the "net spendable." After working with buyer after buyer, I simply faced the reality that cash flow was the name of the game in the eyes of a professional real estate buyer.

Another reality was the fact that, contrary to popular belief, most serious professional buyers do not look at "tax loss" as the primary consideration in purchasing properties. Myths about depreciation in real estate have been carefully disseminated over the years—primarily, I suspect, by the "dopers"—but the truth of the matter is that most buyers look at depreciation as "frosting on the cake." The depreciation feature of real estate is an added reason for making this type of investment, but cash flow is still the primary consideration when it comes to income-producing properties (that's why they're called "income-producing" in the first place). I found that whenever an owner spent a great deal of time talking about the "tax shelter" aspects of his property, the chances were good that he did not have a salable piece of real estate. It was my experience that when an owner did have a substantial cash flow coming from his property, he emphasized that fact above everything else.

Another early giveaway to an unsalable property was the owner's putting a lot of emphasis on how much it had cost him to build the project or how well it was constructed. The quality of the construction, while important, was still only "frosting on the cake." And what it had cost the owner to build the project was not even frosting; in fact it was totally irrelevant from the standpoint of a prospective buyer. That latter statement—though hard for builders to understand—is yet another example of hard reality: the market value of a property, from a cash flow standpoint, simply bears no relation to the fact that the owner—for a variety of reasons—may have spent more than he should have when he built the property.

I therefore came to the conclusion that the person

who knew the *least* about a property's realistic value was the owner. I did, however, have to get an indication from him as to his "asking price," even though I knew that he would most likely give me a much higher figure than the one he might eventually accept. I don't recall ever dealing with a seller who proved, in the final analysis, that his original asking price was firm. Even if he really believed that he wasn't going to budge from his original asking price, the chances were that he would compromise once he smelled chips on the table—particularly if he had financial problems (which most pathological builders do).

And speaking of financial problems, I should point out right here that the other major consideration in my determination of whether or not a deal was makable was my assessment of how desperate the owner was (after translating his "builderese" into English). The more an owner needed to make the deal, the better my chances of concluding a sale.

So if the owner's "asking price" was anywhere near the rough market price (selling price) range I had calculated, and assuming that there were no glaring or unusual negatives about the property, I would then be prepared to move ahead.

The reality was that a great number of properties were not salable at *any* price. My calculations usually showed a property to have little or no cash flow, or, in many cases, a negative cash flow; on the other hand, I cannot recall ever having talked to the owner of an apartment development who *admitted* to having no cash flow. The gap between the true facts and the "doper's" facts was usually caused by the fantasy in his "projections" or "operating statements." As a general but very consistent rule, owners are so unrealistic when it comes to vacancy factors, replacement costs, and other expense items that are not readily ascertainable, that I normally considered their projections and operating statements to be virtually meaningless.

Thus, with my trusty electronic calculator in front of me, I would be able to quickly figure out—while talking to the owner on the phone—whether or not there was any chance at all that his property was salable. If there was virtually no cash flow or a negative cash flow, or if his "asking price" was so far above the high end of my estimated market range that it seemed ridiculous, I bid the owner adieu and allowed him to go merrily on his way talking to other salesmen about how pretty his project was, how much it had cost him to build it, or what a good "tax loss vehicle" it provided.

If, however, the property did qualify by my calculative standards, I then told the owner I would have to personally inspect the property "before making any commitment." With this latter statement, I managed, for the third time, to set the stage for the casting of the roles of intimidator and intimidatee before I had even met him. The first time had been when I initially called the owner and suggested I send some information about myself before we discuss his property in detail; the second was when he received the Earth brochure; now I was telling him that I was going to travel hundreds, or perhaps thousands, of miles to personally inspect his property, and that I could not "make any commitment" until I had completed the inspection. Obviously I was "somebody."

When I got to that point—not just finding an owner who was interested in selling, but finding an interested seller who had a *salable* property—my next step was to haul my healthy posture onto a plane and visit the owner in order to find out whether or not I might be willing to "make a commitment."

But as you might have guessed, the real purpose of my trip was to get a commission agreement signed. Just to make sure that I stuck to my vow to never again work on the sale of a property without a signed commission agreement, I carried around a little card with the following poem on it—a card that continually reminded me of a brutal reality:

> **"With a written agreement**
>   **You have a prayer;**
> **With a verbal agreement**
>   **You have nothing but air."**

In spite of all the organization and work I had done up to that point, I still had not even completed the first step of selling: obtaining a product. Anyone can work on the sale of a property, but to have written authorization to do so—an authorization which also spells out the salesman's commission—is another thing altogether. Trying to obtain such a document was the first big test for my philosophy, a philosophy which dictated my stepping onto the playing field rather than avoiding it.

When I visited the owner's city, the big moment had finally arrived—but with one new twist: it was the big moment for the *owner*, not for me. After having been intimidated no less than three times, the owner was finally going to meet the "expert from afar." In addition to the image I had taken such great pains to create, I also found that people, for some illogical reason, are usually more impressed with someone from a distant city than they are with an expert who might be readily available to them right in their own town. As a general psychological rule, I found that the greater the distance I had to travel to visit an owner, the more of an "expert" I became.

And when I arrived I was completely equipped with what you might call a portable office. As I do with most everything, I hoped for the best but assumed the worst when it came to the owner's ball park. I assumed that he had one of those old hand-operated calculators that chugs out answers at the blistering rate of one per hour; I assumed that he had a manual typewriter whose keys were so hard to push that it could only be operated by a female Olympic hammer-throwing champion; I assumed that his copying machine consisted of a few sheets of worn-out carbon paper; and I also assumed that his secretary was the normal kind who would break into hysterics if anyone dared to ask her to do something over. In general, I assumed the owner ran his operation like a guy who finds it a complex problem to chew gum and walk at the same time. Every now and then I was pleasantly surprised, but more often than not my assumptions turned out to be correct.

I therefore not only brought my own calculators, pens, typing paper and other supplies and equipment (including, many times, one or more electric typewriters), but I also traveled with at least one, and sometimes two or more, secretaries.

Close your eyes now and try to picture the setting:

Here was a real estate developer who for laughs had long enjoyed such knee-slapping pastimes as pounding bamboo shoots under real estate salesmen's fingernails, throwing bones in the middle of a group of ten or twelve starving co-brokers, and any number of equally enjoyable "kick the salesman" type torture games. Now he sat in his office waiting for his first big meeting with the "expert from afar" who had already intimidated him no less than three times; after his long wait I certainly didn't want to disappoint him.

I marched into his office, impeccably dressed— the usual black briefcase in hand—and was followed by an entourage of anywhere from one to three assistants carrying calculators, extension cords, mortgage rate books, and a variety of other materials and equipment that might be needed. This was the coup de grace, and as a result I was usually in complete control of the situation from that point on. The main reason for bringing my traveling office with me, as I've already pointed out, was to be certain that nothing was left to chance. As a bonus,

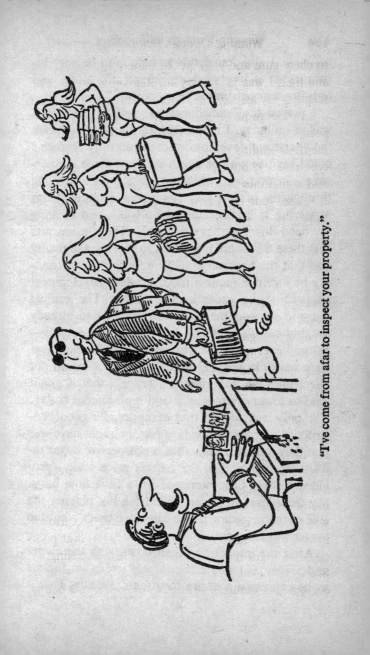

"I've come from afar to inspect your property."

however, I also found this technique to be very intimidating; it improved my image still more, and thus further contributed to my posture.

I played the "noncommittal" role to the hilt. I was in no hurry. I had to see all the facts and look the apartment development over carefully "before I could say one way or another." First came my personal inspection, which consisted of strolling through the project and doing such exciting things as staring at bricks, tapping on walls, and sticking my head down garbage disposals. The illusion was that these things are important to experts; the reality was that the physical aspects are strictly of secondary importance (unless the apartment development happens to be exceptionally tacky). The critical thing to me was the cash flow, and I had already roughly calculated that—in a matter of seconds—before I ever made the trip. Even if the development were built like the Taj Mahal, I knew it would not affect the cash flow numbers (except that it might tend to lower maintenance and replacement costs). The only significance that exceptionally good construction or other secondary factors might have was that they tended to influence a prospective buyer toward the high end of the market price scale—provided he was first interested on a cash flow basis. My technique, however, called for my playing the role of the inspector to the hilt since that's what the owner was anticipating.

After the inspection I'd sit down with the owner and review as many other largely irrelevant factors as he expressed a desire to discuss. Finally, I went into the "open-heart surgery" phase of my technique. The object of this operation wasn't a heart, but the problem of seeing whether or not a deal could be worked out. Instead of asking my assistants for syringes, gauze and scissors, I would have them vigorously slap mortgage rate books, scratch pads and pens into my hand. Sometimes—out of the corner of my eye—I would catch a glimpse of the owner's mouth hanging open as I reached my hand out to the side—without looking up—and called for one of my "surgical tools."

After madly punching away on my portable electronic calculator and thumbing through rate tables profusely, I'd finally look up and say something like: "I'd be able to do something with this property at around 'X' dollars over the mortgage." I didn't say that I could "sell" the property—that would be too gauche; I said I could "do something" with the property. They mean essentially the same thing, but as I've previously pointed out, phrasing is extremely important from a psychological standpoint. Saying that I could "sell" the property would have made me sound like "just another broker;" by phrasing it the way I did, I remained the mysterious "expert from afar." This is a good example of how the difference between just two phrases can mean the difference between being intimidat*ed* or being intimidat*ing*.

The first figure I threw out to the owner was usually at the low end of what I had calculated the broad market range to be, thus I became accustomed to receiving a negative response. Oftentimes, however, this brought the owner down considerably from the original, and usually unrealistic, "asking price" he had quoted me over the telephone. After the owner threw a "counter-figure" back at me, I would then shake my head slowly from side to side, mumble, open my rate books once again, and start punching away on the electronic calculator. Many mumbles later I'd look up and say something like: "Hmmm, I see where my mistake was the first time. I guess I could go about 'Y' dollars on the property." I jockeyed around like this with the owner until I felt I had the price down as low as I could possibly hope to at that early stage of the game.

Then I whipped out my file of pre-typed contracts (which I never called "contracts") and said something to the effect of: "I like to keep things simple, so I just use a one-page 'understanding' to summarize each of my deals." Again, whether a document is called a "contract" or an "understanding" does not have any legal significance, but psychologically it's very important—"contracts" scare people.

This was the first really delicate point between ground zero and the pocketing of a commission. If I failed to get the owner to sign the understanding, I had wasted a lot of time, energy and money for nothing. However, even if I succeeded in getting him to sign it, the only thing I had accomplished was obtaining a product to sell—just the first of "the five steps of selling." Up to that point my abstract power (image) had been supporting my posture; now I needed real power (legal tools) to keep my posture strong. And to have legal power it was essential that I succeed in getting the owner to sign the "understanding."

I considered this to be such a critical step that I took the trouble to develop, over a period of time, a whole series of "understandings" in an attempt to cover every type of situation. I did not use an attorney to help me construct these understandings, but instead developed them myself. There were two reasons for this:

The first was simply that I didn't want my understandings to look too "legal." Lengthy, complicated looking documents—particularly ones containing a lot of legal terminology—scare people. If a document was too legal looking, the owner might want to bring his attorney in to review it. And once the attorney stepped into the picture, I knew from past experience that I might just as well pack up my rate books, calculators and secretaries, and return from whence I came. I went into every deal assuming that there was a deal-killing attorney waiting in the wings behind the owner. While I knew that I'd have to come face-to-face with that attorney if and when it ever came time for a closing, there was no way that I wanted to go up against the monster problem-finder before I even had a commission agreement signed.

The second reason I wrote my own understandings was that I wanted to make them just as practical as they were legal. "Practical Law" isn't taught at Stanford U., Harvard U., or any of the other more prestigious universities; it is taught only at Screw U. And, as you've already seen, I was fortunate enough to have had some great practical law professors during my undergraduate days at that realistic center of learning. In fact, each sentence I included in my understandings was inserted specifically to avoid a replay of some previous beating I had received during my undergraduate days. I eventually ended up with a series of about twenty contracts, but it never ceased to amaze me how those Type Number Ones, Twos and Threes always seemed to manage to come up with new, ingenious ways to try to do me out of my chips.

Because of the brevity and lack of legal terminology in my agreements, plus the fact that I had firmly established myself as the intimidator, I was usually able to get the owner to sign on the dotted line without summoning his deal-killing attorney into the picture. I always considered it crucial to get the agreement signed quickly during that first meeting, while the posture my image power had given me was still very strong. In getting this accomplished, two key things about my technique were very important:

The first was that I tried to get as much information as possible over the telephone so that the blanks in the agreement—with the exception of the asking price—would be completely filled out prior to my arrival at the owner's office. The second was that in the event some changes did have to be made in the agreement, I had a fully equipped office traveling right along with me.

I developed these two unorthodox techniques specifically to avoid fumbling around at the crucial moment and thereby blowing my chance to get the agreement signed. No matter what business you're in, you can certainly see where you could use similar techniques to your advantage, with perhaps just a few adjustments to more specifically orient them to the problems that you most commonly face.

If the seller did sign the commission agreement, then, notwithstanding the fact that I had already invested a tremendous amount of time, energy and money in the deal, I still had only accomplished the first of five steps. The analogy I could use is that it was about the equivalent of having just received the ball and starting out first-and-ten on my own 20 yard line—80% of the field still had to be covered.

Chapter 11

Advancing To Midfield
Is Relatively Easy

Translation: *Locating a market is the least difficult step.*

So as not to be misleading, let me emphasize the word "relatively" in the title of this chapter. While it's true, compared to the other four steps of selling, that I found the location of a market (serious, interested buyers) to be a relatively easy step, it still took a great deal of time, effort and money to accomplish.

The main reason why this was the least difficult step is that it's to a buyer's advantage to look at as many deals as possible; and since he normally has no obligation to the salesman regarding a commission, he generally welcomes any submission that a salesman wishes to send him. However, in order to find the right buyer for each property, and to gain the respect and, hopefully, support of that buyer, the salesman must still have a workable technique.

Just as I began Chapter 10 by explaining the reality that working with other salesmen should be avoided when soliciting deals, the first thing that I'll point out about real estate "buyers" is the reality that most of them aren't really buyers at all. Through considerable wasted time, effort and money, I found that most people who claim to be real estate buyers (or buyers of *any* big "product," for that matter) seldom, if ever, actually close a sale. Just as sellers are continually able to suck salesmen in to working on unmakable deals, I also observed that many salesmen are repeatedly lured into wasting a great amount of time and effort talking to "buyers" who never actually buy anything.

I can't imagine a more sadistic situation than a well-meaning but naive salesman trying to sell an unmakable deal to a non-serious buyer. Any salesman who gets himself into that kind of situation ends up feeling very much like a ping pong ball, with the would-be seller and non-serious buyer being the paddles. If you're one of those people who needs an occasional bit of sadism to spice your life, I suggest that you anonymously send an unmakable deal, along with the name of a non-serious buyer, to some real estate salesman whom you particularly dislike. You'll find this to give you more enjoyment than high black boots and a whip.

How do you spot a non-serious buyer? Well— again using real estate as an example—you first have to understand that even though a company or individual is listed in a publication as a buyer, that doesn't mean that it's a *serious* buyer. Secondly, even if an entity is a large public company or real estate trust, that doesn't mean that it is actively involved in the purchasing of properties. The vast majority of public companies and real estate trusts listed in various real estate publications are primarily engaged in building their own properties or making interim mortgage loans, or else they're involved in specialty fields such as hotels or nursing homes. Of those that *are* primarily interested in purchasing properties, a great majority of them, at any given time, are "out of the market" (not currently interested in purchasing additional properties because they have no more cash available, have problems with their existing properties, or a variety of other reasons). So even though the names of real estate "buyers" are readily available to any salesman, there is considerable work to be done in qualifying those "buyers."

I finally learned to spot non-serious buyers because they all tend to talk and behave in the same manner, regardless of the type of business they're in. In real estate, if you ask a non-serious buyer about his guidelines for buying properties, he'll most likely tell you that he "has no guidelines"—that he is "interested in looking at anything." On the other hand, most serious buyers have definite guidelines because they know exactly what they're looking for. Another consistent tip-off is the fact that when you submit a deal to a non-serious buyer, he tends to dwell on questions of secondary importance, such as those pertaining to location, construction, and/or age of the project. As I previously pointed out, such questions are normal, but not until the buyer is first satisfied with the numbers and has decided that he has a definite interest in purchasing the property. Serious buyers get down to the nuts and bolts right away; they understand the mathematical guidelines for evaluating the key factor in income-producing properties—cash flow.

You might wonder why a non-serious buyer would continue to encourage salesmen to submit properties to him. The reason for this is that the non-serious buyer takes an attitude of "everything to gain and nothing to lose." Even though he is not seriously interested in purchasing properties, he figures that it's still always a good idea to know what deals are floating around. Also, there's no telling when he might accidentally run across a "steal" (a property that is so good, at a price so low, that no one can pass it up). But if I were ever lucky enough to work on a "steal" (I never was, by the way; I'm not so sure that there really is such a thing), I certainly would not be in need of non-serious buyers; my serious buyers would be happy to gobble it up.

In order to locate serious buyers, I used a technique similar to the one I used for finding makable deals. My initial problem was to learn what types of properties each buyer was interested in, and also what his general guidelines were for analyzing those properties. Once again my approach was to make sure that everything I did enhanced my posture.

I had much less trouble getting buyers to speak with me over the telephone than I did property owners, simply because, as I said, it's to the buyer's advantage to work with as many salesmen as possible. Also, since the buyer normally has no obligation to the salesman regarding his commission, he usually takes an ostrich attitude on the subject of the salesman getting paid; buyers find it convenient to hide their heads in the sand when the seller starts to cut off the salesman's hand. The famous, standard line of the buyer is: "The commission is between you (the salesman) and the seller; I don't want to get involved." If you're a real estate salesman, that last quote probably struck a familiar chord. In most cases it might be appropriate to describe it as "premeditated apathy." (Day in and day out you can view apathy—*premeditated* apathy—all around you, in all walks of life; just take a good, hard look.)

My initial purpose in calling a buyer was to find out what his guidelines were so I would not waste a lot of time sending him information on properties that did not meet his qualifying standards. Even though a buyer was more than happy to receive submissions, I knew he would not be receptive to answering questions for a real estate broker over the telephone. Therefore, just as I had done with the owners of properties, I took the initiative and suggested that I first send the buyer some information about myself and my method of operation. Into the mail would go my Earth brochure, again followed up by a telephone call a week or so later. As with the sellers, the reaction was that I must be "somebody."

When I called the buyer for the second time, I was not "just another real estate broker" in the pack; I was the mysterious "expert from afar" who used a $5 brochure as his calling card. During this second call I explained that since we were both (the buyer *and* I) very busy people, I thought it would save a lot of time if he would answer a few quick questions so I could avoid sending him properties that didn't fall within his guidelines. Already having a strong posture at this point because of the image I had created, I was usually able to get the buyer's cooperation on this request. For purposes of recording this information, I developed a "Buyer Information Form" which, when properly filled out, allowed me to quickly determine whether or not a given property fit a certain buyer's objectives.

And the very first question on the form was quite unusual: Was the "buyer" a principal or broker? The reality was that not only were most of the entities listed as real estate buyers actually non-serious buyers, but many of them were primarily interested in acting in the capacity of brokers when it came to selling properties.

As an example, a large construction company might have been listed as a real estate buyer even though it had never bought a property. The president of that company, however, might just happen to have been a licensed real estate broker who took other salesmen's deals (submitted to him because of his company's misleading classification as a "buyer") and submitted them to serious buyers, hoping to share in a commission.

I found that a common naivety among salesmen is their failure to understand that no matter how wealthy a "principal" might be, he is never too rich to be above earning a nice little real estate commission, or "finder's fee," on the side. (And, once again, this applies to *all* types of businesses.) Because of the shock value of my unusual first question, I found that the buyer would normally—by reflex action—tell me the truth or, at the very least, stutter around enough to make it obvious to me that he was, in fact, primarily interested in acting as a broker. And if I did become convinced that he was just a broker fronting as a buyer, I eliminated him from my buyer list.

But if the buyer "got by" that first question, I would then breeze through the rest of the form in a minute or two. The more deals I submitted to a buyer and the more I talked to him about why those deals were not of interest to him, the more specific I was able to become in adding additional information to his form. More importantly, after a reasonable period of time I was able to tell whether or not he was actually a serious buyer. And I'm sorry to say that my firsthand experience showed that the vast majority of entities listed as real estate "buyers" are not really buyers at all; they are either brokers or "curiosity seekers." (Curiosity seekers infiltrate every business and every walk of life, and in order to make any headway in this world you must be able to weed them out and avoid being impressed with their variety of intimidating disguises.)

What I finally ended up with was a very small but very valuable hard core group of serious buyers, buyers with whom I developed good personal relationships. It's somewhat of a paradox that even though a salesman technically works for the seller in most cases, it's the buyers with whom he has the continuing relationships.

I found that most of my buyers fell almost right on the line between it being and not being in their best interest to see me receive my commission. In theory, at least, a buyer can purchase a property for a lower price if the seller does not have to pay a commission; in that respect, he does not have the salesman's best interest at heart. On the other hand, since the relationship is potentially a continuing one, and since a serious buyer wants to look at as many deals as possible, it is in his best interest for the salesman to be happy.

And when it comes to a buyer determining how valuable a continuing relationship with a salesman is, the deciding factor is how well the salesman does his job. That's why I considered it important to have a strong posture in the eyes of the buyer, as well as in the eyes of the seller. Ideally, I wanted each buyer to consider me to be so important to him that he would drop the normal modus operandi of premeditated apathy and insist upon my being paid at the closing. Unfortunately, I never quite reached that extreme with most of my buyers, although the majority of them usually at least gave me their moral support. Even that was very valuable, though, because a salesman who has both the buyer and seller against him is a very lonely salesman indeed.

Before going on to the third step of selling, I'm going to give you a true-life example of what can happen to a salesman when he doesn't have the support of the buyer. It was a case where I had all the legal tools going for me (a real estate license in the state where the property was located, a signed commission agreement with the owner, and plenty of certified mail), yet still lost my chips.

The buyer involved in this particular sale was primarily a builder, but he had recently put out the word that he was also interested in purchasing existing apartment developments. I paid a personal visit to this Florida builder in order to find out if he was really serious about acquiring existing projects. He assured me that he was, and he gave me some rough guidelines to go by. Shortly after that I sent him, by certified mail, a presentation on some apartment properties in Houston which carried a total asking price in the area of $10 million.

Then a curious thing happened. From out of the blue I got a call from a total stranger who said that he was "associated with" the Florida apartment builder whom I had visited. (I should have been sophisticated enough by that time to know that vague expressions such as this are almost always a sure sign of trouble.) He emphasized that he was not an employee of the Florida builder, but an independent principal who had the responsibility of reviewing all deals for the builder, for which he in turn received a participation in any properties they acquired. I said I *should* have been sophisticated enough to recognize that something was wrong, but, unfortunately, the reality is that no matter how sophisticated you are, there's always another creature in the jungle who can think of an entirely new gimmick for getting your chips—and this was one of those gimmicks.

The story is a long one, but I prefer to make it short because it's painful. Oversimplified, I did the usual first-class job in presenting the property and following through with my marketing techniques. My follow-through, however, was not with the builder, but with his "associate." I even went to the expense of flying the "associate" to Houston to inspect the properties, and I spent a lot of time wining and dining him. For weeks I was assured by the "associate" that "they" were still working on the deal, but I finally assumed that the Florida builder was not a serious buyer; I woke up one day to find that my assumption had been entirely wrong—the deal had already been closed without my knowledge.

Why did I not sue the seller when I had all three legal tools in my possession? It was because of my understanding of practical law; consider the following:

1) First of all, both the buyer and seller claimed

that they had been talking to each other about the properties before I had registered the buyer with the seller. In other words, not only did the buyer not offer me moral support, but he was actually siding with the seller.

2) Secondly, the buyer refused to accept any responsibility for the actions of his "associate," saying that he had never authorized the "associate" to represent him. Though he was "nice" about it, his position, in effect, was that it was my tough luck if I had been taken in by someone who claimed to be representing him.

3) Thirdly, the "associate" in turn claimed that I had somehow "misunderstood" what he had said to me, and that he had never told me he was "associated with" the buyer in the first place. This fell into the jungle category that I refer to as **The Big Lie.** No matter how sophisticated or experienced you are, you can never be fully prepared to cope with anyone who is willing to go the whole route—to tell The Big Lie. Regardless of the legal tools you might have on your side, if you sleep with big dogs, you'll most certainly end up getting big fleas.

4) Fourthly, even though it was obvious to me that this jungle trio had succeeded in putting Ringer through the wringer, I was realistic enough to realize that there was just enough confusion surrounding the facts (because of the involvement of the builder's "associate" and the fact that the buyer was siding with the seller) to give some smart litigation attorney sufficient ammunition to confuse a judge or jury.

5) Fifthly, our court system is the number one tool jungle creatures have at their disposal for offsetting proper legal tools. Because of the time involved in bringing something of this nature to trial, the guy in the wrong always has the advantage. After some investigation, I concluded that it would take anywhere from three to five years for the matter to be settled in court, and in the meantime I would not only have to come up with considerable cash to pay legal fees and other costs, but I would also have to invest additional time and energy while allowing myself to be further aggravated in the process.

6) Sixthly, the coup de grace was that there was a strong rumor that the seller of the properties might have to declare bankruptcy (supposedly the proceeds of the sale were not nearly enough to bail him out of all his troubles); and after investigating this rumor I became convinced that his bankruptcy was a definite possibility.

When I weighed all of these facts it just didn't seem worthwhile to pursue "justice." I had already learned over the years that the jungle has its own set of rules for applying "justice": If you lose your case in the jungle, you lose your case . . . *period*.

So even though the buyer doesn't normally pay the salesman's commission, and even though the salesman technically works for the seller, I felt it was very important to also have good techniques for developing solid relationships with the buyers.

At the point in time when I had obtained a product to sell and had at least one proven, serious buyer whose Buyer Information Form indicated that he might have an interest in the type of property I was offering, I then considered myself to have accomplished step number two: locating a market for my product. Down on the playing field I estimated that I had advanced the ball to perhaps the 50 yard line; at that point I still had a long, long way to go.

Intimidation willing, though, I might just make it.

Chapter 12

I Reached The Opponent's
20 Yard Line Through
Proper Execution

Translation: *The quality of my marketing method was crucial in advancing me to the point of closing.*

As you may remember, before graduating from Screw U. I had decided that I not only wanted to have abstract and real power supporting my posture on future deals, but also performance power. I wanted to be so good at my job that I would have total credibility with the buyer and seller, as well as with a judge or jury if I ever had to take court action to collect a commission.

After considerable research and development, I worked out a unique system for gathering information and preparing presentations, which I felt—on the basis of firsthand comparison—were as good or better than any I had previously seen.

My information-gathering technique was not only geared to provide detailed, accurate data, but it was also constructed in such a way that a person with very little knowledge of real estate could properly implement it. Just as I had managed, through experience, to develop commission agreements which became more and more sophisticated, I also developed a series of "Property Data Forms" to fit almost every conceivable type of situation.

I was able to teach several secretaries, who had no previous real estate training, to correctly use these forms. Gathering the information required by the form was a very time-consuming job, but one which, because of the way the form was constructed, didn't take a great amount of real estate knowledge to perform. I therefore did not have to stay around for another day or two after obtaining a signed commission agreement from the owner of the property; I could leave one of my secretaries behind to gather the necessary information, thus freeing me to work on other deals. (Once again, I don't know of any type of business where the development of good systems, for the purpose of delegating authority with a minimum of errors, is not crucial.)

After my secretary gathered all of the information (which in some cases took several days to accomplish because of the complete lack of organization on the part of the owner), she then returned to my office and submitted her completed form to a "presentation girl." Like everything else in my operation, the technique I used in putting together my presentations was developed and improved over a period of time. During the latter stages of the evolution of my Property Data Form, as well as the evolution of the style used in my presentations, the two came to correspond almost exactly.

In other words, the presentation, in effect, would consist of a neat, detailed version of the Property Data Form—the conversion of the material contained in the Property Data Form into a neatly typed package which was easy for the buyer to review. When the presentation was completed, I would then review my Buyer Information Forms (the one-page form discussed in the previous chapter) and decide who the best prospects were for that particular property.

After selecting these prospects, I would then be prepared to put into effect my third legal tool: certified mail. I considered certified mail to be the potential savior—the ribbon around my package of legal tools. In the event of having to go to court to collect a commission, if my real estate license and commission agreement were not enough, then evidence in the form of certified letters might prove to be the deciding factor. This was an example of recognizing and acknowledging reality—the reality that I might have to take legal action to collect a commission, even though I hated lawsuits and would do just about anything to avoid the time, energy, aggravation and expense of suing someone. It was another example of hoping for the best but assuming the worst. By making that assumption I lost nothing if the "worst" never developed; on the other hand, I was one step ahead if the "worst" did come to pass.

So I sent the presentation by certified mail to each prospective buyer who I thought—based on his Buyer Information Form—might have an interest in the property.

Was I perhaps getting a little too carried away with my defensive measures? You decide for yourself after you read the gory details of each of the six deals I describe in Section IV. All I was doing was recognizing, acknowledging and dealing with reality. In actual fact, the future was to teach me that no matter to what extremes I went to guard myself in the jungle, I was always *under*-protected.

About a week after I sent a presentation by certified mail, I would call the recipient to see if he had an interest in further pursuing the matter. If he was not interested, I would try to learn specifically why, so that I could note the reasons on his Buyer Information Form. If, however, he indicated that he did have an interest in the property, I would then register his name with the owner by certified mail. At that point I could say that my civil defense was in great shape.

My next major objective was to get the prospective buyer to meet the seller and inspect the property as soon as possible. Everything I did was geared toward this objective, so part of my technique called for getting all of the necessary information quickly flowing back and forth between the buyer and seller. Of course, my primary objective remained the same: to receive a commission. Therefore my technique for keeping a steady flow of information existing between the buyer and seller—like all of my other techniques—was carefully devised to be in harmony with my central objective. Because of the fact that my posture was excellent in the eyes of both the buyer and seller, I was normally able to keep the lines of communication flowing through me rather than around me. Long distance telephone calls were also important because they became a matter of official record and, if ever needed, could help to substantiate the degree of my involvement in the making of a sale. (I don't care if you're in the business of selling tuxedos to Aborigines, it will pay you to keep in mind that the long distance portion of your phone bill is a permanent, irrefutable legal record; you never know when some flaky Aborigine might decide to tell The Big Lie, and it could very well turn out to be that the appearance of his phone number on your telephone bill becomes the deciding factor in exposing T.B.L.)

If a buyer ever mentioned to me that he would like to speak directly with the seller—or vice versa—I handled it in a method designed to add to my strong posture. Rather than displaying nervousness

over such a request—which would have denoted
weakness—I immediately indicated that I thought it
was an excellent idea (even though I really thought
it was a horrible idea) and told (not asked) the
buyer or seller, whichever the case might be, that I
would set up a conference call among the *three* of
us.

The key to the technique I used in handling this
was that I neither hesitated nor asked; I responded
immediately, stating with authority how it was
going to be handled. Dealing from a position of
strength, I was bold and took the initiative. This
was yet another specific technique for applying the
key ingredient of my philosophy—intimidation—to
my specific business and *my* specific objective within that business.

I knew that if I allowed the buyer and seller to
talk to each other directly—without my being on
the phone—I would be asking for my first posture
puncture. And posture maintenance is a funny
thing: no matter how slight that first puncture may
be, it's usually malignant in nature; it spreads rapidly. So I always tried to tactfully discourage any
direct conversation between the buyer and seller,
acknowledging the reality that private communication between them could be the beginning of a
whole series of events—all negative.

There was only one thing more dangerous than
the buyer and seller speaking directly with each
other over the telephone, and that was their meeting
face-to-face without my being present. Of course I

didn't need to worry about that possibility until I had the buyer interested enough to spend the time and money to travel to the seller's city.

My feeling about getting the buyer to inspect the property was very much like that of an insurance salesman who feels that he's three-quarters of the way toward making a sale if he can just persuade the prospective client to take a physical examination. I felt that if I could motivate a serious buyer enough to take the trouble to get up from behind his desk, board an airplane, and fly to a distant city in order to meet the seller and inspect his property, I was then rapidly approaching scoring position. Obviously a sale was never going to take place until the buyer made such a trip, because even though he could determine his initial interest based on a handful of relevant figures, there was no way that he was going to get serious about a closing until he had personally met the seller and stared at a few bricks.

My technique called for two specific procedures in order to hurry the buyer's decision to hit the road:

First of all, I practically spoon-fed the prospective buyer any information he requested. I tried to remove as much responsibility as possible from everyone else involved in the deal. As an example, if there were "legal" questions about the mortgage, instead of spending several days trying to track down the seller's attorney and then waiting several more days for him to get back to me with an answer, I would undertake to dig out the required information myself. I trained one of my secretaries to read and understand the relevant points of mortgages, mortgage notes, deeds of trust, mortgage commitment letters, and most other documents involved in real estate closings. It often happened that a secretary was able to obtain the answer to a buyer's "legal" question in fifteen minutes, thus avoiding the inconvenience of having to wait a week or two to get the answer from some attorney who was too busy trying to kill someone else's deal to give us a quick answer. It wasn't a matter of me or my secretaries practicing law, but just a case of our taking the initiative and digging out required information from the mortgages and various other documents.

Likewise, if an "accounting" question came up I called the seller's accountant only as a last resort. Again, one of us could often resolve the "accounting problem" in a matter of minutes, whereas it might have taken a week or two to track down the accountant and get an answer.

The second procedure I used in trying to speed up the buyer's decision to visit the owner was to continuously impress upon him my belief that all of his questions could be answered at one time if he would just meet with the seller and personally inspect the property. Each time I obtained another answer for him, I reemphasized the point that a trip might save him a lot of time in the long run. If he was a serious buyer and had a definite interest in purchasing the property, the logic in my suggestion usually seemed to have a positive effect.

There was a definite reason why I felt it was critical to bring the buyer to the point of deciding to personally inspect the property, that reason being explained by the

FIDDLE THEORY

This theory, like the others, applies not only to real estate deals and not only to selling in general, but to just about everything in life. And man, is this theory ever based on experience—all bad.

The Fiddle Theory states that the longer a person fiddles around with something, the greater the odds that the result will be negative. In the case of Nero, Rome burned; in the case of a sale, the longer it takes to get to the point of closing, the greater the odds that it will never close. As a general rule, you should assume that time is always against you when trying to make a deal—*any* kind of deal. There's an old saying about "striking while the iron's hot," and my experience had taught me that it certainly is a profound statement in that circumstances always seem to have a way of changing.

In real estate, the critical change can be any one of a number of things. The mortgagee may decide, for a variety of reasons, that it wants an unreasonable fee in exchange for allowing the property to be transferred to another owner; the seller's wife may talk him out of making the sale; or the buyer may close another deal and decide that he doesn't want to make any more purchases for awhile. The Fiddle

Theory simply acknowledges reality—the reality that circumstances are constantly changing.

The only thing that I could be sure would not change was my desire to collect a commission, so I didn't fiddle around. Not only did I not argue about whose responsibility it was to get which facts, but, on the contrary, my objective was to undertake all of the responsibility possible. I could not count on how anxious the seller was to sell his property or how anxious the buyer was to buy it, but I could certainly count on how anxious I was to receive a commission.

The Fiddle Theory is an adjunct to the Tortoise and Hare Theory: I always trudged ahead relentlessly—hoping that the other guy would momentarily relax—because I knew that if I didn't fiddle around, I might get "there" a minute, an hour, a day, or a week earlier, which could mean the difference between making and not making the deal.

So by trying to assume as much responsibility as possible for answering questions and gathering information, and by continuously suggesting to the prospective buyer that he could probably have all of his questions answered at one time if he'd personally visit the owner, I was able, in many situations, to speed up by several weeks the buyer's decision to personally inspect the property. And once he made that decision, I felt I was getting pretty close to scoring territory.

Whenever possible I would make arrangements to come to the buyer's city ahead of time so that we could "review the details of the deal on the plane" on the way to the seller's town. What this really did was give me the opportunity to make sure that the buyer and seller didn't meet before I arrived, and it also gave me the chance to develop a more personal relationship with the buyer. In addition, the buyer, seeing me once again going above and beyond the normal call of duty, would—hopefully—begin to feel some sense of loyalty to me. At best I was hoping to bring our relationship to the point where the buyer would not go through with a closing if there were any hanky-pank regarding my commission; at worst I was hoping to at least bring our relationship to the point where the buyer would feel very uncomfortable and embarrassed at being a party to a situation in which he knew that I was being deprived of my commission.

In cases where I did not accompany the prospective buyer on his flight to the city where the property was located, I met his plane at the gate when it landed. Any way you sliced it, I was always right there between the buyer and seller, taking the initiative in discussing the various aspects of the deal. And just as important, I knew what I was talking about when I spoke—because I was prepared.

In previous years I had also known what I was talking about, but it hadn't mattered because my posture had been wrong. Now my posture was right. It was right because of my image power and legal power, and I was now backing it up by demonstrating "execution (performance) power." I wanted to display so much knowledge about the property and the making of the deal that even the seller

"I could swear you look different than when I saw you in New York, but I can't seem to put my finger on what it is."

would be embarrassed to challenge my right to a commission (naive and wishful thinking on my part, I might add).

My chief objective was to get all of the buyer's questions answered in order to bring the buyer and seller at least to the point of roughly structuring the terms of a sale, but I also concentrated on accomplishing one other thing: seeing to it that the buyer and seller were never together without my being present. At that particular phase of the sale, The Tortoise imitated Mary's Little Lamb—*everywhere the buyer went, I was sure to go*. When all of the buyer's questions had been answered and, hopefully, a deal had been structured, I personally accompanied him to his departure gate at the airport. (I never left town first, even if it meant missing my last flight out and having to stay overnight.) Not until the buyer's plane had pulled safely away from the gate did I shed my lambskin and revert back to being a tortoise. I cannot over-emphasize the fact that a technique similar to this one is a near necessity in every business I can think of.

At that point, if everything had gone as planned and the buyer and seller had verbally committed themselves to going ahead with a sale, I had successfully accomplished step number three: implementation of a marketing method. I then considered myself, for the first time, to be in scoring position; I would say that I was at perhaps the opponent's 20 yard line. I could smell pay dirt for the first time. I had not yet won, but I was in the process of doing so . . . through intimidation.

As everyone knows, however, moving the ball those last 20 yards is a son-of-a-gun; that's where the defense stiffens and the going really gets tough.

Chapter 13

Scoring

Translation: *Closing the sale.*

Invariably, shortly after a buyer and seller came to general agreement on the terms of a sale, a strange thing would happen. After the seller had spent months trying, without success, to stir up buyer interest in his property, would-be "purchasers" suddenly started beating a path to his door. All at once, like magic, everyone wanted to buy his property. It was downright amazing.

This phenomenon occurred with such frequency that I finally began to count on it happening in every deal. Heeding the Theory of Reality, I acknowledged it as a fact of life and used it to my benefit, rather than allow it to work against me. I made myself look smart by assuring the seller in advance that this phenomenon would occur. I told him not to be overly impressed with himself or his property when it did happen, as it was a normal occurrence in every deal. I explained that he should not take such "offers" seriously, because if these soon-to-appear "buyers" really had legitimate interest in his property they would have previously made offers to him. So when these questionable "offers" did begin to come in, it just added to my already strong posture; it served to reaffirm in the buyer's mind—and rightly so—that I knew what I was talking about. This is another example, once again, of a specific technique for keeping the flow of intimidation on your side of the fence, even in the face of what appears to be a negative.

It's interesting to analyze what caused this sudden onslaught of "offers" to appear each time I was about to close a sale, because the psychology behind it very much affects the lives of all people—not just those in the real estate business. The motivating force behind it was the reality of two theories, the

BOY-GIRL THEORY and BETTER DEAL THEORY

The Boy-Girl Theory is probably the most basic of all psychological rules governing human relationships. In fact it was in existence the day man first appeared on earth. It states that every person wants what he *can't* have and does not want what he *can* have. It is most evident in the "boy-girl game," and

"Ooh, Hunchy, you're such a brute."

there are very few adults in this world who have not played that game. It works like this:

If boy plays it cool, then girl wants boy (or vice versa); if boy comes on like hungry dog chasing squirrel, then girl doesn't want boy (or vice versa).

If you've ever seen a guy who looks like the Hunchback of Notre Dame walking down the street with a gorgeous female on his arm, and wondered what the girl could possibly see in him, you were undoubtedly viewing the results of the Boy-Girl Theory; the old Hunchback probably knew how to play it cool. The same psychology applies in business. No matter how important a man may be, he'll usually want the deal he *can't* have and won't want the deal he *can* have. If there has ever been a reality that a salesman or businessman—or anyone, for that matter—could use to his benefit instead of allowing it to work against him, the Boy-Girl Theory is that reality.

Because of this, the nearer a deal got to the point of closing—the point where it would become "unavailable"—the more other "buyers"—both serious and non-serious—imagined they wanted it. The property that had always been available was suddenly being taken out of circulation; the "girl" who had always been around was about to get "married." In most cases, of course, this sudden surge of "offers" amounted to nothing more than a panicked reaction to the elements of the Boy-Girl Theory on the part of other salesmen and "buyers." As a result, most of the offers were pie-in-the-sky in nature. Since other salesmen had absolutely nothing to lose by tossing out "offers" to the owner, I could usually count on several of them beating a path to his door and making a "better offer" from some mysterious "client" as we neared the closing.

I might also point out that the Boy-Girl Theory worked against me in another way. The nearer we got to a closing, the more the seller thought of it as a deal he could have, and that, of course, was bad from my standpoint because the Boy-Girl Theory would then be negatively pushing from both ends: not only did other "buyers" suddenly start imagining that they wanted the property, but very often the seller would begin thinking that he didn't want *my* buyer's offer because it was a deal he knew he could have—it was "available."

As to the Better Deal Theory, it states that before a person closes any kind of deal—including marriage—he always worries about the fact that there may be a better deal down the road. It holds just as true if the "deal" involves insurance, vacuum sweepers, or even the acquisition of a hundred million dollar company, as it does for selling real estate. It's an uncontrollable instinct: at the last moment, the thought has to at least occur to a person that he might be missing out on a better deal somewhere else.

Because of this, the seller's mind was always open to the last minute pie-in-the-sky offers that were sure to be directed at him. He was the perfect pigeon because he was already worrying—at least subconsciously—that if he closed my deal he might miss the opportunity for a better price on his property later on. So when those other salesmen came busting through his door at the eleventh hour and tossed out higher "offering prices" from mysterious "clients," the seller's mind was ripe—he *wanted* to believe that the "offers" were for real. The result was that his imagination got carried away and he started to take seriously offers that he normally would recognize as having no substance. In this respect, then, these last minute "offers" were primarily a figment of his own imagination.

To combat the negative effects of the Boy-Girl Theory and the Better Deal Theory, my objective was to do everything within my power to bring the deal as quickly as possible to the point where the money was on the table and the papers were ready to be signed. If I could reach that point, it was then " put up or shut up time"—time for all of the mysterious "clients" to put up their money or crawl back into the woodwork. Rarely did they do any "putting up," and consequently the seller would usually begin to question if there really was "a better deal down the road" after all.

Once the chips were on the table, the Boy-Girl Theory would begin to have a reverse effect in my favor because a serious buyer doesn't leave his cash lying around on the table forever. The more a seller hesitated, the more the buyer would then show signs of having second thoughts about the closing himself. And when that happened, the seller usually began to have a better appreciation for the deal he might be losing if he didn't get on the stick and get it closed. When he saw signs that indicated he might be about to lose the "girl," he then started realizing just how badly he had really wanted "her" after all. And the fact that the boys in the bleachers hated to see the property being taken out of circulation didn't really matter anymore since they had failed to "put up" when my buyer's chips were on the table.

Two things I did to endeavor to bring the deal to the "put up or shut up" stage as quickly as possible were to analyze what the real objectives of the buyer and seller were, as well as analyzing their real objections. I say "analyze" (rather than "find out") because it's been my experience that parties to a deal very often don't know what their real objectives and objections are (just as successful people don't always know the real reasons for their success). Also, because of a variety of ulterior motives, either the buyer or seller, or both, might purposely suppress their real objectives or objections.

The two objectives of which I could always be absolutely certain were that the buyer wanted to buy the property for the lowest possible price and the seller wanted to sell it for the highest possible price. That is the epitome of a conflict of interest, and it's precisely what selling is all about; if there were no basic conflict of interest between the buyer and seller, there would really be little need for salesmen. The better a salesman is at being able to resolve this conflict, the better his chances of earning (but not necessarily receiving) commissions.

If I were able to correctly analyze and satisfy the basic objectives and objections of the buyer and seller—including the basic conflict over price—the most important thing I could then do to help effect a quick closing was to once again take on as much responsibility as possible. The Fiddle Theory was always foremost in my mind: once the buyer and seller had spelled out the deal—"agreed to agree"—I knew that time was of the essence; one extra week, one extra day, or even one extra hour might mean the difference between making and not making the sale.

As I had done in implementing my general marketing method, I tried not to depend on the performance of any of the other parties. From the moment the buyer and seller "agreed to agree," my entire office was available twenty-four hours a day. There was no way that I wanted my commission to depend upon the performance of the buyer, the seller, either of their attorneys or accountants, and most certainly not upon the performance of one of their "executive secretaries" (most "executive secretaries" I've known are the type who might send a critical document across the country by mule train instead of hand-carrying it to the airport post office and sending it via Air Mail Special Delivery). My technique was such that I considered some documents to be so important that I would have one of my secretaries personally fly to one city to pick them up, then fly to another city and hand-deliver them. Once I was inside the 20 yard line, the stakes were big enough—and the odds against a closing had decreased sufficiently—to make it worth my while to risk considerable money in order to prevent unnecessary delays.

My technique often astonished the buyer and

seller's employees. I almost got the impression that they had never heard of Air Mail Special Delivery, let alone telephones. I found life to be very uncomplicated for many of these people: if someone requested certain information, it was understood that you merely gathered it at your leisure, put it in an envelope, applied a first class stamp, and dropped it in a mail box at the end of the day. After all, sending something Air Mail Special Delivery could cost nearly a dollar; and to pick up the telephone and call the information in to someone—in order to save the three or four days that it might take for a letter to arrive—could cost two or three dollars; of course, to spend the money to get on an airplane and hand-carry a document to another party was just total insanity—only a tortoise would be crazy enough to do such a thing. (But I might add that I can't think of a business in which this technique, or one similar to it, would not increase the odds of winning in your favor. You must—no . . . change that to: you MUST—take matters into your own hands and move swiftly once you smell victory. This applies just the same whether you're trying to win a business deal, a football game, or a woman. When it gets down to the crucial moment, the great quarterback always takes control of the game.)

As usual, I also tried to make certain that I was a party to all telephone conversations between the buyer and seller, and definitely made every possible effort to attend any meetings between them, no matter how costly or inconvenient it might be for me to do so.

Finally, if all went well I succeeded in advancing the ball to the one yard line—the point at which the chips were on the table and the documents ready to be signed. But that last yard can sometimes be tougher than the previous nineteen. My education at Screw U. had taught me that when I arrived in town for the long-awaited closing, there were still two potential major obstacles that could keep me from getting that last yard—from scoring.

The first and most awesome obstacle was the **Attorney Goal Line Defense.** There's no goal line defense any better than this one; there is no way that any attorney worth his salt is going to just sit back and allow a deal to close without at least putting up a fight.

There we were—the buyer, the seller and me—all in the same room, chips on the table and the deal ready to close. Predictably, at that point, who should enter the scene? Not Superman, not Plasticman, not even Cookieman—no, it was none other than **Legalman.** Onto the field he would dash, flapping his Brooks Brothers cape in the wind and cackling as he opened his briefcase full of little deal-killing goodies. Would this be an easy one to kill, he wondered? Would he be able to knock this deal off without working up a sweat? Or would this one be a challenge?

The seller's attorney would immediately put into effect the "he-we-I" evolution. At the outset, Legalman would talk in terms of "he" (the seller) in discussing the property and the closing; then in a relatively short period of time, the word "he" would

"I haven't given up a touchdown in the last eight deals, and I
don't intend to start now."

evolve into the word "we" (the seller *and* the attorney). At that point the seller was no longer in full control of his destiny; he and Legalman were then making the decisions jointly. Finally—you guessed it—Legalman turned "we" into "I" (the attorney). At that stage the seller had completely lost control; it was then entirely Legalman's deal. The buyer and seller had been reduced to merely bothersome, but necessary, bystanders to the closing.

Now if the buyer and seller were bothersome bystanders to the deal, can you imagine what The Tortoise was in the eyes of Legalman? He might have considered me to be bothersome, too, but he certainly couldn't understand why I was necessary. Because of this, when Legalman first entered the scene he always seemed confused by my strong posture in the situation. After all, wasn't I "just a real estate broker?" What was I even doing at the closing, anyway? How dare I not be intimidated.

In order to understand how incredible such a situation was to him, you have to appreciate the fact that there are many natural predators in the jungle —animals whose survival depends upon the killing of their prey. One of those predators is the attorney, and he preys upon deals; Legalman's survival depends upon his ability to kill deals, and the creature who spawns those deals is a salesman or promoter— a deal-maker. Now perhaps you can appreciate the setting.

Talk about conflicts of interest: my sole purpose in life was to get the ball over the goal line, and Legalman's training had specifically prepared him to keep just such a guy as me from moving that last yard. And I might add here that if you refuse to face this reality—the reality that most attorneys, at least subconsciously, consider it to be their primary function to find a way to kill every deal—you will never be *totally* prepared.

I should further add that I don't blame attorneys for having this kind of attitude, because it's not their fault; their law school training prepares them for this task in life. A Phi Beta Kappa friend of mine once told me that his law school education consisted, in effect, of three years of learning how to *find* problems; he said that he could not remember even one course that was directed at the *solving* of problems. With that kind of background how can you possibly blame attorneys for being deal-killers?

Since I'm on the subject, I should be fair and also say that not every attorney is a deal-killer. Despite their "education," many of them have managed to break out of this mold, and as a result I'm happy to say that there are actually a number of "deal-maker" attorneys throughout the world. Unfortunately, however, the reality is that these deal-making types are few and far between, so I took the position that it would just be luck if I ever happened to cross paths with one. Therefore, when I got down to the one yard line I assumed that I would be up against a "normal" attorney—one who was effective at implementing the Attorney Goal Line Defense.

I knew that Legalman would expect me to come crashing through the middle of the line and that he'd set his defense accordingly, so my technique was to try to finesse my way over the goal line rather than come right at his strength; with an end sweep or perhaps a lob pass out in the flat, I might just be able to make that last yard untouched. I did not push or try to get tough at the closing; attorneys are not subject to intimidation like buyers, sellers and other normal people, simply because their law school brainwashing teaches them that no one has a higher station in life than a legal counselor. With that kind of self-image, how can an attorney possibly be intimidated?

On the other hand, I also knew that it would be a fatal mistake to cower. If there was one thing that I had to give Legalman credit for, it was his killer instinct. I knew that once he smelled blood—once he sensed weakness on my part—he would immediately move in for the kill. If I took the "Yes, Your Highness" attitude that so many of my comrades in the pack had been intimidated into taking with attorneys, I knew that Legalman would knock the ball right out of my grasp and pounce on it.

I therefore straddled the fence: I was neither tough nor humble; I just played it cool. My attitude was calm and matter-of-fact. When I spoke, it was with an air that indicated there was no concern over the deal—that the fact there was going to be a closing was just assumed by everyone. "Problems" did not represent obstacles to a closing, but just normal "points" which had to be "handled" as a natural part of every closing. That kind of attitude was very confusing to Legalman because he expected me to display at least some expertise in either the art of arguing or the art of cowering. Thus by acting unconcerned about each little deal-killing goody that he pulled out of his bag, I was usually able to throw him off balance and thereby weaken his defense. He was unprepared to deal with someone who refused to even acknowledge the existence of his little bag of goodies.

As Legalman tossed out each of these goodies, my typical response might be something like: "That's a darn good point (not problem); I'm glad you brought it up." I would then proceed to state (not ask) many ways that we (not just Legalman) would (not could) handle (not solve) that particular point (not problem). Never did I challenge Legalman. My whole attitude was simply that it was assumed by everyone that there was going to be a closing and that the only purpose of our all being present was to "handle" the normal "points" that come up at *every* closing.

Legalman had never been up against a tortoise before. Old standby "problems" such as needing a certain document from the mortgagee—problems that Legalman had always been able to count on to stall a closing for at least a week or two (to give the Fiddle Theory time to take effect)—were dissolved before his very eyes by The Tortoise merely dispatching one of his secretaries across the country to pick up the document and hand-carry it back to the closing. After handling a couple of Legalman's best shots in this manner, he might—if I were lucky—begin to tire and decide that the long lunches, golf games and martini hours he was missing by trying to keep this strange tortoise from traveling one lousy yard were not worth it. Hopefully, he would then ease up just enough to allow me to edge the nose of the ball over the goal line.

However, if Legalman would not yield, I then called upon the Boy-Girl Theory as a last resort. The seller had to be pretty inhuman not to be affected by the Boy-Girl Theory. What I would do is take a casual attitude, indicating that the deal was off—something like: "Well, I guess that's it; it looks as though we just can't make this one." If it ever got down to that point, it was then "big boy time" for the seller; it was time for him to assume control once again—to take *his* deal back from Legalman; it was time for him to stand up and let it be known that he was once again calling the shots.

Unfortunately, not many sellers (or businessmen of *any* kind) have the nerve to take such "extreme" action, and about the only thing I know of that can get them that emotionally fired up is the fear of losing the "girl." So if nothing else worked—if there were no other way to handle Legalman's Attorney Goal Line Defense—I still had a remote chance if I could just instill in the seller the thought that he was about to lose the deal—that he couldn't have it after all. Then, as per the Boy-Girl Theory, there was an outside possibility that he would suddenly want it so badly that he'd have the nerve to stand up to Legalman.

Before leaving the subject of the Attorney Goal Line Defense, I should point out that—in real estate, in particular, but in many other types of businesses as well—there is one factor that is even more important than all of the techniques I've just described for overcoming Legalman's little bag of deal-killing goodies. Unfortunately, however, the salesman has no direct control over it. It's the degree of financial desperation on the part of the seller. As you'll see in Section IV, the more desperate the seller, the better the chances that he, out of desperation, will not allow Legalman to gum up the closing.

(I said that a salesman has no *direct* control over this factor, but he does have indirect control over it by virtue of the fact that he has the power to decide which deals to work on. And that all gets back to the subject of working hard to find makable deals rather than working hard to try to make unmakable deals. Aside from the mathematics involved, I would say that the degree of financial desperation on the part of the seller is the single most important factor in determining how makable a deal is. In any type of business, if you pick the right person to deal with—one who has himself stuck way out on a limb financially—you'll be amazed at the help he can give you in traveling that last critical yard at the closing.)

In summation, you *must*—regardless of what business you're in—face the reality, once and for all, that Legalman has been, is, and, unfortunately, probably always will be a major obstacle in almost every sizable transaction that takes place on planet Earth (unless the general population can somehow get it through its head that an attorney is nothing more than a college graduate with a special diploma which grants him the right to openly practice intimidation); and secondly, you *must*—one way or another—develop specific techniques for protecting your deals from the clutches of this blood-thirsty predator.

The other obstacle that usually confronted me at the one yard line was not, surprisingly enough, the buyer's attorney. The reason the buyer's attorney seldom caused insurmountable problems was that his client (the buyer) was in the business of buying properties. If the buyer was a serious professional whose main line of business was the purchasing of income-producing properties, then his attorney had usually been trained—many deals ago—to discard his own bag of deal-killing goodies and to do everything possible to help the buyer accomplish his objective. On the other hand, even though the owner was in the process of disposing of one of his developments, his normal business was not the selling of properties; in most cases it was the construction, ownership and management of apartment developments. With few exceptions, the sale the owner happened to be involved in was an isolated case, more often than not the result of his desperate need for cash; he therefore had never had any reason to "train" his attorney to help accomplish the closing of a sale.

I like to refer to the other obstacle that usually confronted me at the one yard line as the seller's **Dirty Laundry**. That Dirty Laundry could include any one of a number of surprises. Some of the more common ones were the last minute uncovering of undisclosed, major liens against the property (even though the seller had assured the buyer that there weren't any), the discovery that the mortgagee had no intention of allowing the property to be transferred from the seller to the buyer (even though the seller had assured the buyer that the mortgagee had already given approval to the transfer), and the detection of far more vacancies in the apartment development than the seller's "rent roll" had shown (a favorite seller trick is to fill vacant apartments with relatives, friends and employees until after the closing).

If real estate happens to be your game, you have to face the reality that no matter how many times the seller assures you that all of the information he has submitted is correct—that there are no hidden surprises—it's almost a certainty that there will, in fact, be several major undisclosed items—of a deal-killing nature—discovered as a sale nears the closing stage.

What I did was try to soften the blow of the inevitable Dirty Laundry by preparing the buyer for it ahead of time. Just as I forewarned the seller that there would be a sudden surge of phony offers once he had a verbal agreement with my buyer, so also did I warn the buyer that he could absolutely count on many negative surprises as we neared a closing. This not only helped to mentally prepare the buyer for the Dirty Laundry problems, but once again tended to make me look like I knew what I was talking about when they did crop up.

Just as I tried to turn Legalman's "problems" into normal "points" that had to be "handled" as a part of every closing, I also tried to create an atmosphere of expectancy, rather than shock, with regard to the inevitable Dirty Laundry. Hopefully, in addition to my forewarnings, the buyer had enough experience to realize that a seller's surprises are usually both numerous and major at every closing. My objective, then, was to try to eliminate as much of their shock value as possible.

If it could not be eliminated, there were several other maneuvers I could try in order to finesse the ball over the goal line. If the Dirty Laundry was in any way a physical problem—if, for example, it could be solved by sending someone to another city to pick up a document or administer some persuasion—then, following my normal technique of trying to take matters into my own hands, I'd perform whatever physical acts were necessary; however, if the problem couldn't be solved by physical means, there was always the faint hope that I could persuade the seller to lower his selling price just enough to "fairly" adjust for the previously undisclosed negatives; and if that didn't work I tried to see if either a "sale-leaseback" or "contingent payment sale" could satisfy both sides. All else failing, my last resort would be to use the psychology of the Boy-Girl Theory: I would talk to the buyer alone, reminding him of all of the property's good points, and hope to create in his mind the emotional feeling that he was about to lose the "girl."

Of course if the Dirty Laundry was just too ridiculous—as it often was—I then had to reluctantly classify it as a "factor beyond my control." Remember, as I pointed out in the Theory of Sustenance of a Positive Attitude Through the Assumption of a Negative Result, there definitely are factors that are beyond the control of the salesman. Thus no matter how good I was at implementing my techniques, there were deals where I managed to finesse my way around end in order to avoid Legalman, only to have Dirty Laundry stop me with a shoestring tackle before I could cross the goal line. If it was not within my power to negate the effects of the Dirty Laundry, I just had to ultimately face the reality that I could not control the destiny of that particular deal.

But if I did manage to get past both Legalman and Dirty Laundry at the goal line, I then got credit for a touchdown . . . right? Wrong! At that point, I had only completed the fourth step: closing the sale.

After all of the time, energy and money I had spent in obtaining the product, locating a market, implementing my marketing method, and closing the sale, it was still all for naught if the points didn't go up on the scoreboard; if I committed an infraction on the touchdown play, then all of the effort I had expended to move the ball down-field was meaningless. And that's what closing a deal and not getting paid for it is like: scoring a touchdown and having it called back because of a penalty. I knew that I had to become an expert at avoiding a penalty at the last crucial moment, and I also knew that whether or not I was assessed a penalty would revolve around my ability to remain the intimida*tor*.

Chapter 14

Crossing The Goal Line
Becomes A Bore
If You Don't Get Credit
When You Score

Translation: *Getting paid is what it's all about.*

Contrary to much of the brainwashing you may have been subjected to over the years, the object of the game is not to close deals, but to receive satisfactory "compensation" (once again, this could be in the form of love, trophies, money—just about anything).

In real estate, selling a property is only a means to an end, that end being the pocketing of a commission by the salesman. Earlier in this book I explained why I use such expressions as "earn, and *receive*, income"—because there is a big difference between earning and receiving. When I closed a sale, I had only *earned* my commission; all of the techniques I used in performing the first four steps of selling, however, were directly or indirectly geared toward accomplishing the fifth and most important step: getting paid. To make sure that I never lost sight of what the real objective of the game is, I carried another little card around with me which read:

> **"Closing deals is so much trash**
> **If you, my friend, don't get no cash."**

In the first chapter of this book I expressed some dim views about many "success" and "how to" books, but I did not point out the most curious thing of all: I've seen a lot written about doing what's in the "client's best interest," but what about the salesman's best interest? I've seen a lot written about how to obtain a product, how to locate a market for the product, how to implement a marketing method, and how to close a sale. But I don't recall ever reading anything about accomplishing the most important step in a sale: getting paid.

At Screw U. I had come to the conclusion that most salesmen simply put their emphasis in the wrong places. It's wonderful and very "moralistic" to have the client's best interest at heart, but perhaps your wife and kids would feel just a little more secure if you also had *your* best interest at heart. Without reservation, I can honestly say that in all of the deals I ever closed I walked away feeling that I had performed an outstanding service for my client and my getting paid certainly did not change that feeling.

There is no conflict in doing what you agreed to do for someone (in the case of real estate, the buyer) —and doing it well—but also getting paid for it. In selling real estate, I found that the only "conflict" is the one created by the seller when it suddenly occurs to him that if he doesn't pay the salesman the agreed upon commission, then he himself can end up with more chips. All I did was put a stop to allowing the seller to intimidate me into thinking that my only concern should be his welfare and that being concerned about my own needs was in some unexplainable way "unethical." (In every walk of life, one of the most commonly used intimidation ploys is to make a person feel guilty for not "properly concerning himself" with "the other guy's" welfare —experience self-reproach for being so heathenish as to think of his own well-being. A perfect illustration of this is the rhetoric of most so-called "liberal" politicians—and it works for them: they've been winning through intimidation for quite some time.)

Remember what the Theory of Intimidation says: that the results a person obtains are inversely proportionate to the degree to which he is intimidated. I developed techniques for becoming the intimida-

tor, and these techniques gave me a strong posture
—something I hadn't experienced prior to my graduation from Screw U.

They positioned me for the ultimate objective of getting paid. In the final analysis, I guess you could say that the major factor which separated me from the rest of the pack was that I simply oriented my understanding of the power of intimidation toward mastering the art of getting paid.

As a closing drew near, the three most specific things I did to protect the strong posture I had worked so hard to attain were to:

1) Keep my finger on the pulse of the deal so that I could pinpoint the time and place of the closing,

2) Maintain my good relationship with the buyer so that I would at least have his moral support, and

3) Bring an attorney to the closing so that I'd have the unwritten Universal Attorney-to-Attorney Respect Law working for me.

If—despite my strong posture and all my precautions—the seller still tried to cut off my hand when I reached for my chips, then it was just plain old showdown time. Of course he might just attempt to whack off a couple of fingers (reduce my commission) rather than go for my whole hand (not pay me at all), but in either case I had worked too hard to obtain the necessary legal tools to have to resort to bluffing; nor would I allow myself to be bluffed. I abided by the

BLUFF THEORY

This theory states that the best way to bluff is *not* to bluff. You may have noticed that wealthy people are very good "bluffers." My Type Number One Professor at Screw U. had taught me that the reason for this is that rich people, by virtue of their wealth, have staying power. As I previously pointed out, he was always prepared to walk away from any deal because there was no one deal that he needed. My professor's "bluffing" always worked simply because he wasn't really bluffing at all; when he threatened to walk away from a deal, he really meant it. He could not be intimidated; he was always the intimida*tor*.

If the secret to bluffing was not to bluff, and the secret to not bluffing was to have staying power, and, further, if wealth was the very backbone of staying power, then I reasoned that I would have to find a substitute for wealth that would guarantee my having staying power. The substitute I finally came up with was guts. It hurts a bit more than being backed by wealth, but using guts definitely does work. This substitute is as available to you as it is to the wealthiest person. I simply drew an imaginary line and said to myself: "This is where intimidation stops. No more bluffing beyond this line."

If the seller started to reach for my chips, I moved swiftly in an effort to gum up the closing. The secret was to avoid being lulled into fiddling while the horse was getting out of the barn; once the closing took place, my problem would become one of a whole different magnitude if I had not already received my commission. (In the next section you'll see how getting lulled into not taking quick action once cost me more than $65,000.)

If for any reason the seller did manage to get through the closing without paying my commission, and if he refused to do so shortly thereafter, I then had to resort to the one thing I had tried to avoid in using all of my techniques (and particularly in building up my "civil defense") in the first place: a lawsuit. Unfortunately, the inadequacies of our legal system are such that, from a practical stand-point, even the winner of a lawsuit usually ends up losing. But if that were the only course of action I had left, I did not hesitate to take it. I didn't bluff.

However, if everything went as planned I didn't have to resort to taking any legal action after the closing. I could look back over my shoulder from the end zone and see that no penalty flags had been dropped, and I could watch the points go up on the scoreboard. I had then completed the final—and most important—step: getting paid. When it was over I wasn't always the most popular guy at the closing, but after my education at Screw U. I had decided that I would rather have the seller taking my name in vain as I walked away with my chips, than have him remarking what a nice guy I was as I walked away without my hand.

At that point, I could finally say that I had won —through intimidation.

And to show you how it works in actual practice, the next, and final, section of this book is devoted to a blow-by-blow description of the deals I closed during the very first year in which I put my philosophy and techniques into effect. These deals resulted in my actually receiving $849,901 in real estate commissions, yet I was the very same person who had barked for a $1,250 bone just a couple of years earlier . . . with one exception:

I had mastered the art of winning through intimidation.

LEAPFROGGING TORTOISE HITS THE JACKPOT

Translation: My Understanding Of Intimidation Pays Off.

Chapter 15

Like MacArthur, I Returned

Translation: *I returned to Missouri—scene of my worst humiliation—in total triumph.*

Missourians have a saying: "You have to show me." The last time I had ventured into the state of Missouri—almost two years earlier in St. Louis—I went home wagging my tail behind me. I had "stepped out of line" and tried to break precedent; I was the bad boy who had reached in the cookie jar and ended up getting spanked; I had scored a touchdown and dared to suggest that the points be put up on the scoreboard; I was the out-of-step real estate salesman who had closed a deal and then had the nerve to expect to be properly remunerated for my services; I had reached for my chips, and, because of this presumptuous and bold attempt, had gotten my hand cut off just below the wrist.

And it was my horrible experience in Missouri, more than any other, which had prompted me to vow to find a way to change my posture to one of strength. I had promised myself that I would leapfrog to a new level and that I would get paid big commissions in the future. But Missourians who knew anything about the St. Louis fiasco would not have been impressed with my vows; as true Missourians, they would have to be shown.

It was only fitting, then—though strictly coincidental—that less than two years after my worst disaster—the biggest single turning point of my career —I should return to the state of Missouri to stage the scene of my first major triumph. It was also just a poetic coincidence that my second Missouri deal (actually my second and third deals—there were two separate closings in Kansas City) happened to be approximately the same size as my St. Louis sale had been.

I first made contact with the owners (there were three partners) of the Kansas City properties a few weeks before my "leapfrog" discussion with my assistant. As I previously explained, I was in the process of making a commitment to get completely out of the second mortgage business and to organize my philosophy and techniques so that I would never again be intimidated—so that I would be in a position to get paid big commissions. It was also ironic that during the few weeks prior to my assistant's departure from my employ, he had begun to do the leg work on the Kansas City deal.

The best screenplay writer could not have put together a more dramatic script. Had I listened to my assistant's "logic" and "mastered" the second mortgage business before trying to "move up in class," I would never even have pursued the Kansas City deal in the first place. But after my assistant left, I was firmly committed to putting the Leapfrog Theory into action, so I rolled up my sleeves and went to work on the Kansas City properties; and less than two weeks later I made my first visit to the owners.

How different it was than my last experience in Missouri only a short time before. In the St. Louis deal I had been assured by my Type Number Two professor that his "integrity" was "beyond reproach" and that I therefore had no need for a signed commission agreement. Needless to say, when I left Missouri after my first visit to the Kansas City owners, I did have a signed commission agreement and my posture was one of strength.

When I first arrived in Kansas City, I did so with an image as the "expert from afar." After a couple of weeks of analysis and several telephone conversations between me and the Kansas City owners, I finally decided that the deal "looked worthwhile enough for me to gamble my valuable time on"; naturally, though, I would have to personally inspect the properties before I could "make a commitment."

The fact that the eight properties were spread out in small towns surrounding Kansas City—both in

Missouri and Kansas—made my inspection task very difficult. Nothing too good for the "expert from afar," though, so the owners rented a small private plane and I was able to personally "inspect" all but one of the apartment developments within a 24-hour period. When I finished, I was not only bored stiff from looking at garbage disposals, air conditioning units and bricks, but I was also totally exhausted.

Then came the big moment—for the owners, that is. I did some mumbling, punched a few buttons on my electronic calculator, and implemented the rest of my new technique designed to accomplish the "first step of selling." The owners were in luck. The "expert from afar" had been satisfied with the inspection and his calculations had worked out. He indicated that he could "do something" with their properties. And it just so happened that he had eight written "understandings"—one for each property—in his briefcase (with most of the blanks already filled in).

I emphasized that the "understandings" could, of course, be terminated unilaterally at any time, and that they did not preclude the owners from working with other people regarding the sale of their properties. And before you could say, "Pardon me, did you say you were a broker?", the "understandings" were signed and the "expert from afar" had disappeared across the wheat fields of Missouri. Was he for real, or had the owners just been dreaming that an "expert from afar" had descended upon them? Would he return?

You bet I returned—many times. But first there was an important item to be attended to. At that point I had obtained only one of my three legal tools —a signed commission agreement; I did not yet have a real estate license in either Kansas or Missouri. Shortly before I first contacted the Kansas City owners, I had started inquiring about the necessary procedures for becoming a licensed real estate broker in both states. I had already begun working my way through the mass of red tape that had to be dealt with in order to be scheduled to take the real estate broker's examinations, but at the time I signed up the Kansas City deal I had not yet actually taken the test in either state.

Once the eight commission agreements were signed, however, I knew that I had to take the time and trouble to quickly do whatever was necessary to obtain these licenses. After all, it was right there in Missouri that I had learned my hardest lesson: that a seller is under no obligation to pay a real estate commission to someone who doesn't have a real estate license in the state where the property is located.

So in the weeks following my initial visit to Kansas City, while I was working hard to interest prospective buyers in the deal, I had to take time out to travel to Jefferson City, Missouri (have you ever tried to get there?), and Topeka, Kansas, to take the required licensing tests. I passed both examinations and shortly afterward received my real estate brokerage licenses. Unlike my previous Missouri experience—in which I had had none of the legal tools

—this time I already possessed two of the three legal tools necessary to give "real" power to my posture.

From the very beginning of the Kansas City transaction, I was gearing myself to the ultimate objective of getting paid. I was putting my emphasis in the right places; I wasn't off in the clouds somewhere, hoping to get my thrills by being able to tell people that I had *closed* another multi-million dollar deal. I had already experienced *that* kind of thrill before but it hadn't helped pay my grocery bills. This time my emphasis was on making sure that I walked away from the closing with both my hand *and* my chips. As a result of putting my emphasis in the right places, my posture remained strong throughout the entire deal.

Immediately after my first trip to Kansas City, I worked night and day putting together neat, detailed, accurate presentations on the eight properties, then sent them (by certified mail, of course) to a number of prospective buyers whose Buyer Information Forms indicated that they might have an interest in this type of deal. Approximately four weeks after that initial visit to Kansas City, the owners received a certified letter from me wherein I registered the eventual purchaser of the properties.

After many telephone conversations with both the buyer and sellers, the buyer finally indicated that he was interested enough to travel to Kansas City to inspect the properties and see if a deal could be made. After going through the exciting process of "inspecting" the properties once again—this time with the prospective buyer—we all sat down to see if we could structure a deal.

The discussions were fruitful, and when the buyer and I left Kansas City (need I say who left first?), the three of us (the buyer, the sellers *and* me) had come to a general "agreement to agree." Unlike so many nightmares of the past, it was not just the buyer and sellers who had come to an agreement, while that unnecessary nuisance—the salesman—panted outside in the reception room. I had taken charge from the outset, and every step of the way my emphasis had been on those things that would ensure my staying in charge—which in turn would help me to obtain my ultimate objective: getting paid.

Yes, it was the *three* of us who had verbally "agreed to agree."

I had noticed from the very beginning that the prospective buyer (actually it was a public company, but for convenience I'll refer to the head of that company as the "buyer") was extremely anxious to make the deal. His company had come out of nowhere over the past year or so, making several impressive property acquisitions. In looking through its annual report I was able to see that if the company purchased the eight Kansas City properties, the general effect would be to elevate it from a relatively small, rapidly growing firm to a major corporation in the real estate industry, almost overnight.

I therefore sensed that it was the right deal, in the right place, at the right time . . . and that I was the right guy, in the right place, at the right time. To me it was the Packers on the Dallas six inch line—in 15-degree below zero weather—with six seconds to go; it was Truman giving 'em hell from the rear of his train at showdown time; it was Bogart putting the dame in her place at the crucial moment.

First you have to be prepared; then you have to have the opportunity; lastly—but most important—you have to *come through* at the moment of truth. Everyone has plenty of these opportunities in his lifetime, but all that counts is whether or not a person takes advantage of them. I had had such opportunities in the past, but had blown them because I wasn't prepared. But now I was ready. I would not be intimidated, because I was now dealing from a posture of strength; my image was right and I had all three legal tools safely locked away in my files.

In addition, I was performing. I had already done an outstanding job in securing the necessary information about the properties and presenting it in a first class manner, and I was now properly following through. Was it possible, I wondered to myself, that it was meant to be that I should return to the scene of the worst "crime"—Missouri—to prove, for the first time, that I understood the winning principle of the wealthy—intimidation—and that my new philosophy was workable? Could there be such justice?

After a couple more weeks of hammering out the details via telephone, we all (again, me included) decided that it was time to meet in Kansas City and attempt to finalize the terms of a sale. So back we went to the "show me" state, only this time there were three additional parties involved in the transaction. The new additions were the sellers' attorney, the buyer's attorney, and—you guessed it—The Tortoise's attorney.

By this time nothing that the "expert from afar" did was astonishing to either the buyer or sellers. However, it was a little difficult for the attorneys of the buyer and sellers to fathom the idea of a real estate broker being represented by an attorney at the meetings.

I went through the formality of properly acknowledging all of Legalman's normal deal-killing goodies as "points" that certainly would have to be "handled" so that we could get on with the closing. When appropriate, I stated (not asked) many ways that we (not just the sellers' attorney) would (not could) handle (not solve) the particular points (not problems) in question.

I had a little outside help going for me in trying to finesse my way around Legalman (in this case a very outstanding legal technician, by the way). As I pointed out, I had noted from the beginning that the buyer was over-anxious because this was an opportunity to elevate his company many steps up the ladder by closing just one deal. The result was that he had been talking about a price that I considered to be very much in excess of the market value, at least from a projected cash flow standpoint. (Interestingly, though, the price we had been discussing was still considerably less than the original asking price of the principals, which only emphasizes the point I made earlier about a seller never giving his true price at the outset.) The sellers were smart enough to realize that the price we were talking about (in the area of $2,700,000 over the mortgages) was a once-in-a-lifetime opportunity, and this made them anxious sellers even though they were not financially desperate.

Even so, they were outstanding salesmen themselves, and, like all "respectable" sellers, they continued to cry the blues and complain about the price all through the negotiations. However, their actions spoke louder than their words; though they put on a good show, their desire to close the deal was a big factor in offsetting the Attorney Goal Line Defense. I always felt sure that behind closed doors they were pressuring their attorney to finalize the sale as quickly as possible, even though, for the benefit of the buyer and me, they were giving Oscar-winning performances of dissatisfaction.

I enjoyed studying the salesmanship techniques of the sellers, and to this day I still admire these men very much. I always felt secure with these three partners because they were what you might classify as "nice" Type Number Ones. Right from the beginning they let me know that the name of the game was to get the best deal for yourself that you possibly could, and I respected them for their candor. But whether or not a person is "nice" is in no way related to whether or not he is a Type Number One, Two or Three; what's important is the fact that a Type Number One is the safest kind of person to deal with, regardless of whether or not he happens to be "nice." As I explained earlier, if you're prepared and go in with your eyes wide open, then a legitimate Type Number One is the least threat to you. You have the advantage of knowing exactly where you stand with him, and can act accordingly. It was because of the fact that I could easily spot the sellers as Type Number Ones that I was able to see their "dissatisfaction" as nothing more than a good salesmanship technique.

The negotiations and legal work went on for three days, night and day, until everyone was walking around in a stupor from mental and physical exhaustion. On the second day, as strong as my posture was—and even though I had my attorney present—the principals and their attorneys began, ever so slightly, to perform the usual "commissiondectomy" on me. (Those of you who sell real estate for a living are no doubt familiar with the commissiondectomy. It is the surgical removal, primarily by the seller, of all or any part of a commission from the salesman. Sadly, many salesmen practically volunteer for this operation by leaving their commissions unprotected and exposed to the brutal elements of the jungle.)

It was pointed out to me that the buyer and sellers were still several hundred thousand dollars apart —with no apparent way of being able to resolve the difference—and that the only way the deal could be put together ("of course") was for me to be more "reasonable" with regard to my commission. I assured all of the parties involved that I was not interested in becoming a commissiondectomy patient, which, although it seemed to surprise everyone, did not appear to overly concern them. And I felt pretty certain I knew why.

They all knew I had two legal tools in my bag—signed commission agreements and certified mail—but they also "knew" that I certainly did not have real estate licenses in Kansas and Missouri. Although I'll never have any way of knowing for certain, I think that both the buyer and sellers just assumed that the "expert from afar" wasn't licensed in the two necessary states. How could he possibly be? It would have been unheard-of for anyone to spend the time and money—or have the foresight—to go through all of the red tape necessary to apply for real estate brokerage licenses in two far-off states, study the real estate laws of those states, and then travel thousands of miles to take examinations and get licensed. There is no question that their assumption was more than reasonable. It *would* have been unheard-of for anyone to do it—unless, of course, that anyone was a relentless tortoise who had undergone a major commissiondectomy in that exact same state less than two years earlier.

I've always had the feeling that between the second and third days of our "closing meetings" in Kansas City, the sellers' attorney went through the "formality" of checking with the Kansas and Missouri Real Estate Commissions just to confirm that I was not a licensed broker in either state. All I know is that the atmosphere changed considerably when we met on the third day. Here they were—in the midst of what everyone thought was a perfectly rou-

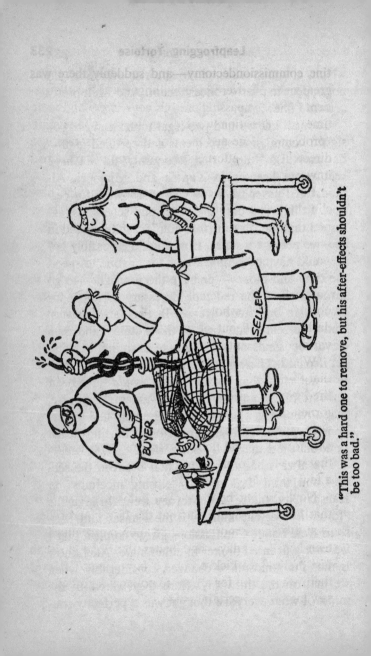

"This was a hard one to remove, but his after-effects shouldn't be too bad."

tine commissiondectomy—and suddenly there was great concern over my unwillingness to be the patient. With the passing of each hour, more and more time and attention were given to the commission "problem." More and more of the conversation was directed at my attorney and me, but we remained unwavering.

For three days the normal negotiations and hassling had been going on. The attorneys had been working into the late hours of the night—and sometimes the early hours of the morning—getting into order the massive legal detail involved in the sale of eight major properties. Typewriters had been clicking away madly, copying machines running continuously, and a whole variety of people had been dashing in and out of the attorney's office to sign various documents.

When we finally stopped working at the end of that third day, it was 2:00 a.m. and we were a very tired group of people. The sellers, the buyer, my attorney and I all went back to the motel where we were staying; then, as we climbed the stairs on the way to our second floor rooms, the buyer suggested that we all go to his room "to relax and kick around a few points."

Now I might be a tortoise, but I'm not so slow that I couldn't figure out that the buyer and sellers —at two in the morning, after another grueling sixteen-hour workday—had better things to do than just "relax and kick around a few points." If ever there was a time for a man to collapse into bed and saw logs, it was certainly then.

So when the buyer made the suggestion that we go to his room, I said to myself: "This is it. You've waited a long time for this moment—almost two years. You've gone through a lot of frustration, agony and humiliation, but in typical tortoise fashion you kept trudging ahead. You analyzed, planned, then followed through. This time you're prepared. It's obvious now that the ball is going to go over the goal line; whether or not you get credit for the score is all going to boil down to whether or not you make the mistake of allowing yourself to be intimidated at the last moment, get 'penalized,' and thereby have the touchdown called back . . . or you play it cool, remember that the only way to bluff is not to bluff, and do the right thing rather than yield to the temptation of doing the instinctive thing and becoming intimidated." Up until then, nothing about the deal had happened by accident, and I wasn't about to let any accidents occur now. As I walked through the doorway into the buyer's room, I was indeed prepared.

(Before describing what took place in the buyer's room, I should point out that there was another significant factor in this deal. In addition to the approximately 1,250 apartment units that made up the eight properties, the buyer and sellers were entering into a contingent agreement for the buyer to purchase nearly 1,000 more units which were supposed to be completed in the near future. The answer to the question of whether or not I, as the licensed real estate broker who had brought the buyer and sellers together in the first place, would also be entitled to a commission on these additional properties—if and when they closed—was unclear. When I had originally discussed the eight properties with the buyer, I had also pointed out to him the possibility of purchasing additional units to be built in the future. Technically, therefore, I had also "presented" the additional properties to him. However, up until the meeting in his motel room, everyone involved, including me, had avoided talking about where I stood with regard to the "to be built" apartments.)

After we were all in the buyer's room, the sellers went through a continuation of their Oscar-winning performances about how much of their own cash they had put into the building of their apartments (during a drinking session many months after the closing, they laughingly told me how they had, in fact, more than "financed out" when they built the projects), and how they would barely get anything out of the sale under the present circumstances. The buyer made it clear that he had already gone much further in price than he should have (and by the way, he was absolutely right), and appealed to my rationality. There was no way that the deal could stand a $375,000 commission (3% of approximately $12½ million). Surely I would not blow up the sale by refusing to accept a commission in the range of $150,000 to $200,000. Why, that was more than any broker in history had ever made on a deal, wasn't it? It was the moment of truth that comes, in one form or another, in every game of love . . . every game of business . . . every game of life:

To be intimidated or not to be intimidated?—that is the question.

Even though I had a posture of strength—a good image and all of the legal tools on my side—the buyer and sellers were still counting on my sanity and logic. Surely I would not be "crazy" enough to throw away the opportunity to earn a handsome six-figure commission; surely I could see the logic in taking a $150,000 commission as opposed to nothing. But the buyer and sellers didn't know about my undergraduate days at Screw U.; the buyer and sellers didn't know about my previous experience in Missouri; the buyer and sellers didn't know that I had waited almost two years for this exact moment to occur; the buyer and sellers didn't know that everything had been carefully planned by me and that nothing in this deal had happened by accident; and, above all, they didn't know that *I* knew it was the right seller, and the right buyer, in the right place, at the right time.

This was the perfect situation, and I was well aware of it. It was time to put it all on the line; it was time to bluff by not bluffing; it was time to go for the touchdown—the whole ball of wax—and not be intimidated into settling for a measly field goal; it was time to show my staying power by using guts in lieu of wealth. I had the unwavering determination of a kamikaze pilot; I had taken my stand and there was no backing down now. After repeated attempts to make me "come to my senses" had failed, the buyer and sellers started to get upset. Timing is always critical, and I knew that the time was right—the setting was perfect—for the now "historic" **Ringer Briefcase Address.**

In a calm manner, I said, "Boys, it's very late and we're all tired. There's no sense going around in circles the rest of the night, because it's obvious that we can't work the deal out. Let's just write this one off to experience; it's not the last deal in the world." I then looked at the buyer and said, "I'm working on a lot of other properties. Sooner or later I'll find you a deal where the mathematics can be worked out." Then I turned to the sellers and said, "As to your properties, I've been talking to several other prospective buyers about them, and I'll try to start cranking up some serious interest in the next couple of weeks."

With that I put my papers back in my briefcase, closed it, then snapped the two latches and center lock shut—very slowly—one at a time. I rose, smiled pleasantly and calmly, started toward the door, glanced back over my shoulder, and, in the most casual manner, said, "Get some sleep. I'll be in touch with both of you in the next couple of weeks." I was completely conscious of the fact— every second of the way—that I was practicing the ultimate in intimidation by reciting the Ringer Briefcase Address. My desire to win was really intense.

I'll always remember the distance. I was approximately three feet from the door when the buyer and sellers yelled out, nearly in unison, "Wait!" That was the most telltale word I had ever heard spoken.

That one word confirmed that I had been right all along—that it was the right buyer, and the right seller, in the right place, at the right time.

I imagine what the buyer had really meant by that one word was that there was no way, after all the work he had done, and after being that close to accomplishing his objective, that he was going to miss the opportunity to propel his company into a major real estate firm overnight just because some real estate broker was crazy.

As to the sellers, the word "wait" probably was their way of saying that there was no way, after all the work they, too, had done, and after being that close to accomplishing their own objective, that they were going to miss the opportunity for a once-in-a-lifetime profit of over $2 million just because some real estate broker was crazy.

After being halted from my near departure from the buyer's motel room, I said that I'd give it one final try. Unbeknownst to either the buyer or sellers, in my own figuring I had looked upon any future commission on the "to be built" units as a bonus, should I be lucky enough to receive anything at all for the sale of those contingent properties. First of all, I knew there was at least some reasonable argument as to whether or not I was even legally entitled to a commission on the apartments yet to be completed. And secondly, I never had any faith in contingent closings to begin with. How did I know if the properties would ever be built, and even if they were, how could I be sure that the buyer would ever complete the sale?

Once again I confirmed that there was absolutely no negotiation regarding my 3% commission for the sale of the eight properties that were going to be closed immediately. "Just as a matter of trying to help pull the deal together," though, I said I'd be willing—"ever so reluctantly"—to take an *additional* $50,000 cash right now in lieu of any future commission on the units to be completed and purchased at a later date. In other words, I was going to give the sellers (and theoretically the buyer) the opportunity to "save" two or three hundred thousand dollars in the future by coming up with "just" an extra $50,000 cash right now.

When the buyer and sellers came out of the ether, the commission we finally agreed to "compromise" on was $426,901.39—about $50,000 *more* than the $375,000 commission I had been hoping to receive all along. That kind of compromising made up for a lot of past commissiondectomies.

Like MacArthur, I had returned. Unlike MacArthur, all I had wanted to do was return to another *opportunity* as big as the St. Louis deal; I had no idea that I would actually return to *Missouri* soil to make good on my vows. It was a great ending for what could have been a terrific script for a movie; fortunately for me, however, it wasn't a script—it was real life. For the first time, I had experienced the thrill of winning through intimidation.

I'll always remember driving over the old bridge that separated downtown Kansas City from the airport, with my commission safely locked away in my briefcase. My attorney looked over at me and asked, "Well, how do you feel?"

Without hesitating, I looked at him and replied: "Deserving."

Chapter 16

It Was So Good For My Health,
I Went Back For Seconds

Translation: *I returned to Kansas City for the second closing.*

The second Kansas City sale should not be confused with the contingent purchase of the "to be built" apartments that I described in the previous chapter (as far as I know, that contingent sale—as is the case with most contingent sales—never closed). The reason that I've discussed the Kansas City deal as two separate sales is because that was the way the buyer and sellers actually ended up structuring it. Four of the properties were closed as one sale, for which I received a commission of $221,446.50; the closing of the second group of four properties, however, did not take place for nearly two months, and since I would never have received my additional commission of $205,454.89 had it not closed, I considered it—as did the buyer and sellers—to be an independent transaction. And as you'll see in this chapter, many problems arose—as they do in every deal—which nearly kept the second Kansas City sale from closing.

A couple of things, in particular, happened between the first and second Kansas City closings which were significant:

First of all, much of the Dirty Laundry that normally comes out just prior to a closing did not show up until after the sale of the first group of Kansas City apartments was finalized. With each new surprise, the buyer became more and more upset with the sellers and, consequently, more hesitant to close the sale of the second group of apartments.

About two weeks before the scheduled second closing, the buyer's attorney sent a letter to the sellers' attorney saying that before there could be another closing, the problems regarding the first four properties would have to be resolved. He enclosed a copy of a letter from the buyer, wherein he (the buyer) had listed no less than 29 unexpected (and unpleasant) surprises that he had discovered since taking over the four properties. In fact, he pointed out that "due to time limitations" no inspection of the fourth property had even been made as yet—the 29 problems involved only three of the four projects. I suddenly had visions of my additional $205,454.89 commission going down the drain with the sellers' Dirty Laundry.

The very next day, the buyer's attorney sent still another letter to the sellers' attorney, this time indicating other serious problems—but of a legal and tax nature—that he had discovered. I reasoned that the buyer's attorney was suddenly reaching into his bag of deal-killing goodies because the buyer wanted to back out of the second closing. I therefore did the only thing I could: I lived on the telephone night and day, relaying information back and forth between the buyer and sellers, using every psychological tool I could think of to try to keep peace between them. Both parties became quite heated as the days passed, and I knew that nothing has a way of dissolving deals more easily than the "temperatures" of buyers and sellers.

The sellers made it clear to me that they felt they had a valid purchase agreement with the buyer for the second group of properties, and that they were going to start a massive lawsuit against his company if he did not go through with the second sale as planned. In trying to get your way, I knew that the worst approach in the world is to make hostile threats to someone, so I urged the sellers not to openly threaten the buyer with a lawsuit for fear he'd get his back up and feel that he had to "stand up to them." Many good deals have been lost over just such a mistaken approach. If you push a man to the point where he feels that he's been challenged, then realities, values and logic suddenly don't matter anymore. I told the sellers that I would set up a conference call with the buyer, and that if we all kept calm and worked together, the "points" in question could be "handled."

I then called the buyer. I told him that even though the sellers were great guys and were certainly honorable, it seemed inevitable to me—"even though they had not yet mentioned the possibility"—that Legalman would suggest filing a lawsuit against the buyer's company if the second closing did not take place as planned. I told him that he should consider such a possibility, because it could be a great blow to the image of his company if it happened. I pointed out that the first Kansas City purchase had given him a great deal of favorable publicity, and that the public was taking note of the fact that his company was growing by leaps and bounds. I said it seemed to me that with his stock climbing as it had been, the possibility of a major lawsuit, with all of the attendant bad publicity, could knock the props out from under the market price of his stock and prove to be a hindrance in his attempt to acquire other large properties.

I assured him that the sellers were reasonable people and that the "points" he had discovered since the first closing could easily be "handled" with all of us working together. I also assured him that the sellers wanted very much to work everything out, and that they were prepared to do anything that was fair and reasonable. I then told him that I was going to set up a conference call with the sellers so that we could proceed with ironing out the details.

That conference call was the turning point. My prefacing conversation with the sellers and buyer apparently had been worthwhile, because there was an absence of hostile talk; in fact, the conversation was very constructive. We went over each of the 29 points one at a time; where there was disagreement, compromise was reached. It was finally agreed that as soon as the sellers had taken care of the items they had promised to correct, the second closing would take place. Within a week, both sides were ready to close, although the closing itself did not take place for another four weeks because of some personal conflicts of the buyer.

One other significant thing happened between the first and second Kansas City closings. My analysis of my experiences at Screw U. had apparently been correct, because the Leapfrog Theory had worked; my planning had been right and I knew that I was prepared. And I wasn't going to rest on my laurels now. I had leapfrogged over the rest of the pack, and I now wanted to go even higher—so high that each future closing would be even smoother than my first Kansas City sale in terms of receiving a commission.

And higher I went—about 41,000 feet, to be exact. That's how high a Model 24 Learjet flies, and I bought one. (Previously, I, like most everyone else, had been intimidated and brainwashed into thinking that it took an enormous amount of cash to buy something as awesome as a Learjet—that only the "wealthy" could afford one. By this time, though, I knew better.)

My arrival for the second Kansas City closing was a real life enactment of every real estate salesman's wildest fantasy. This was one time that I did not fly with the buyer to the seller's city, nor did I even arrive in Kansas City ahead of the buyer. By the day of the closing, both the buyer and sellers knew that the "expert from afar" had purchased his own Learjet, and I had made arrangements ahead of time to meet them at the Kansas City airport.

The buyer and one of the sellers were sitting in the coffee shop at a table next to the window, where they had a clear view of the main runway of the airport. There they were, drinking coffee and waiting for—of all people—the *broker* to arrive. That fact alone set a new precedent in the history of real estate brokerage.

But that wasn't all. Suddenly, from out of the clouds came a shining blue and white Learjet, its jet engines screaming through the skies as it descended toward the runway. The buyer and seller watched as my Learjet touched down and taxied over to a private aviation hangar. The "expert from afar"— who was really nothing more than a good real estate broker who had learned the art of intimidation— had arrived. The closing could now proceed. Need I say that there were no late-night motel room discussions this time? The closing went smoothly and I walked away with another $205,454.89 as my commission for the second phase of the Kansas City sale.

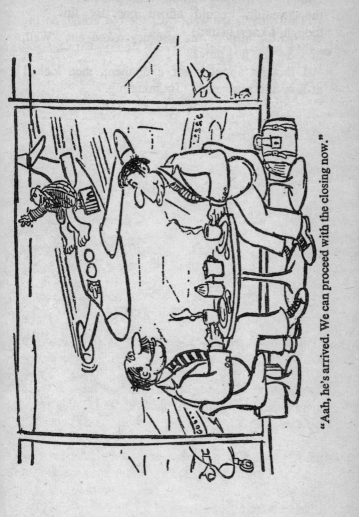

"Aah, he's arrived. We can proceed with the closing now."

This time as we went over the old bridge on the way to the airport, my attorney asked me, "Well, how do you feel *now?*"

I thought about it for a moment, then looked at him and answered: "Intimidating."

Chapter 17

The Tortoise Dons
Hare's Clothing

Translation: *I was lulled into relaxing and paid
dearly for my mistake.*

After the Kansas City textbook illustration of the
use of specific techniques for applying my philosophy to a specific objective, I became perhaps a little
overconfident and deviated from my techniques—relaxed just enough—to get burned once
again. It was obvious from the beginning that the
main principal in my Dayton sale was a full-blooded
Type Number One, so shame on The Tortoise.

The Dayton deal was difficult right from the outset because I put a tremendous amount of work into

just getting my commission agreement signed. After several discussions with the principal, he informed me that his property was actually owned by a limited partnership in which he was only one of three general partners. He assured me, however, that he was the "working partner" and was in complete control of the situation. He finally signed my commission agreement, but inserted a handwritten clause at the bottom to the effect that the agreement was not valid unless executed by his two partners. He said this was merely a "gesture of respect," so as not to offend his Washington partner by making it look as though he were entering into a deal without the partner's knowledge. He assured me that the Washington partner would do whatever he asked him to, and also convinced me that even if the Washington partner did refuse to sign the agreement for any reason, he—on his own—had the authority to bind the partnership. He verbally guaranteed me that he would make the commission agreement valid even without the Washington partner's signature, if necessary. He then called the Washington partner and set up an appointment for me.

I flew all the way to Washington and, bringing back some old and unpleasant memories, spent a couple of hours sitting in the Washington partner's reception room waiting for him to see me. I finally asked myself what the hell I was doing sitting there like a second mortgage broker hoping to be thrown a $1,000 bone if I were a good boy. I asked the receptionist if I could use the phone, then called the working partner long distance. I told him that I was getting ready to walk out the door unless his Washington partner talked to me immediately, whereupon he said that he would call him as soon as I hung up.

Sure enough, the Washington partner granted me an audience within a few minutes. I went over the deal with him and explained the agreement, but he said that he'd like to have a day or so "to study it" before signing. He indicated that he could see nothing wrong with the agreement, but explained that he didn't like to rush into things. I was pretty fed up after sitting in his waiting room so long—particularly after having traveled all the way to Washington—so I wasn't about to lower myself any further by pressing him for a decision. I told him to look it over and get back to the working partner when he was ready to sign.

On the way home, one of those unexplainable coincidences happened. During an hour layover at the Pittsburgh airport, I bumped into none other than the third general partner in the deal. (I was never sure what part he played in the association, except that the working partner had told me not to worry about him. For this reason I came to refer to him as the "mystery partner.") I told him that I had just come from Washington, and although the Washington partner had not yet signed the agreement, it was my understanding that he intended to do so shortly. I then showed him several copies of the agreement containing the signature of the working partner and suggested that he may as well sign it since it was not valid anyway until the Washington partner also signed. So after a brief discussion, the mystery partner added his signature to the agreement; at that point, all I was missing was the Washington partner's signature. However, I wasn't too concerned because all of the evidence indicated that the working partner was in full control of the deal, and he had already promised me that he would go through with the agreement even if the Washington partner refused to sign it.

Not surprisingly, after reviewing the agreement for a few days, the Washington partner did refuse to sign, but the working partner followed through on his promise and told me to proceed with working on a sale of his Dayton apartment project, anyway. He deleted the clause he had added at the bottom regarding the other partners' signatures, and then initialed the deletion (later, the mystery partner also initialed it). The working partner explained that he and the mystery partner controlled more than two-thirds of the partnership and that it was therefore valid for them to enter into any agreement they chose to on behalf of that entity.

Even though the agreement was a little shaky, I went ahead and worked on the Dayton apartment development for two reasons: First of all, as I said, it looked as though the working partner was indeed in complete control of the situation (which the mystery partner had confirmed), and it was him I was dealing with. Secondly, I felt legally protected because I was licensed to sell real estate in Ohio and I also knew that I would end up having plenty of certified mail in my files as evidence. (The real estate laws of Ohio, like most states, were such that even without a written agreement the "procuring broker" was still entitled to a commission if the sale closed.) In order for a sale to be consummated, I also knew that the Washington partner would have to sign all of the closing documents, anyway, which of and by itself would serve as proof of his approval of the sale.

I then went to work in my normal fashion, gathering extensive data and putting together an impressive presentation of the property. Shortly thereafter, I interested the same company which had purchased the St. Louis apartment development, and a representative of that company was soon prepared to go to Dayton to make a personal inspection. (Naturally, I had sent the deal to the buyer by certified mail and had also registered "him" by certified mail with the sellers.)

Before doing so, however, the prospective buyer sent the outline of an offer to me and asked that I have the seller sign it if it was acceptable to him. It was a halfway reasonable offer—$800,000 over the mortgage—and I was successful in getting the working partner to accept it and sign the letter. I then sent the offer back to the buyer, and a week later he came to Dayton to inspect the property (the offer was subject to his inspection). It was the usual touring of bathrooms, bedrooms and laundry rooms, looking down garbage disposals, kicking bricks and opening closet doors. When the buyer left, he was interested in going through with the sale, but there were many problems which would have to be worked out.

The working partner—who had indicated to me that he was in desperate financial straits—said that the only way he was interested in going through with the deal was if the buyer would close right away. Therefore, to expedite solving the tremendous number of "problems" involved, the working partner and I flew to New York a couple of weeks later to meet with the buyer. And that New York trip was where I began to get lulled into a false sense of security.

The working partner and I had already become pretty friendly, primarily because he was (according to what he had said to me on several occasions) in awe of the job I was doing in trying to sell his project. He constantly praised me, saying that he had never seen or heard of any real estate broker operating in such a thorough, efficient and aggressive manner. In fact, he lavished so much praise on me that—much like my opponent, the hare—I sat back on my shell by the roadside and thought to myself, "How sweet it is." (And I don't mean to infer by this that the working partner wasn't sincere in his praise, because I really believe that I never did as much work, or produced better quality, on the sale of any property as I did in this case.)

Another reason for our friendship was that I personally liked his candor. (He didn't exactly have a golden reputation, simply because he was an extreme Type Number One who had no qualms about openly doing whatever was necessary to win.) Dur-

ing one of our conversations—when he and I were
talking about business philosophy in general—he
said to me, "Let's face it, in business each guy grabs
his best hold and goes from there; everything else is
baloney." This might have shocked or offended a lot
of people, but not me. Based on everything I had
seen in all my years in the jungle, I knew that what
he was telling me was only reality; it was not the
way I wished things to be, but the way I knew they
really were.

During the New York trip we tied the bow on our
friendship; he continued to praise me and I continued to enjoy his frankness. The significant point is
that I knew, very early in the deal, that I was in bed
with an extreme Type Number One, a guy who had
let me know—in advance—that the name of the
game was to get all the chips you could, by whatever means necessary. Because of this, I had felt relatively safe; I not only had an excellent posture, but I
went into the deal with my eyes wide open. I figured
that I had nothing to fear because I not only had a
real estate license in the state where the property
was located, a signed commission agreement with
the sellers, and plenty of certified mail going back
and forth between me and the principals, but I also
had the advantage of knowing what the working
partner's philosophy was.

What happened, though, was that because I did
recognize I was up against a Type Number One,
and also knew that I had all of the legal tools on my
side, I subconsciously relaxed; I deviated from my

techniques just enough to get my fingers nipped as I reached for my chips.

As the deal progressed, I worked harder and harder and received more and more praise from the working partner. About two weeks after our New York trip, the buyer sent me a purchase contract which I then passed on to the seller. My posture was right and my techniques were working; all mail and communication were going through me. The seller continued to inundate me with praise for the job I was doing, and I must say that the buyer showed great respect for my position in the deal. There seemed to be absolutely no problem. As we got nearer to a possible closing, there was an excessive amount of information which the working partner had to supply; in my usual way, I took matters into my own hands. In fact, in this particular deal I and my staff took care of things that normally could be handled only by the seller's office. I provided rent rolls, tax bills, and a long list of items which required exhausting hours and many long trips for some of my people. Finally, the buyer was ready to close and made preparations to come to Dayton.

The Attorney Goal Line Defense had been almost nonexistent because of the desperation of the working partner. In fact, Legalman probably figured that the only way he could get his own chips was if the deal closed. On the day of the scheduled closing, however, one of the more common Dirty Laundry problems surfaced: the insurance company (mortgagee) refused to allow transfer of the property to a new owner. The people at the insurance

company's Cincinnati office were disgruntled with
the working partner because of delinquent mortgage payments, rent rolls which they had found to
be less than accurate, and a number of other items
they strongly questioned. Here I was on the one
yard line—a commission of approximately $97,000
practically in my hand—and from out of nowhere
the insurance company was trying to gum up the
works by refusing to allow the sale to go through.

What did I do? Again I took matters into my own
hands and flew to Cincinnati with my attorney and
the working partner.

What transpired at the insurance company's office that day was like something out of a soap opera.
The seller begged, but the insurance company people stood firm; the seller begged some more, but
they still didn't budge; my attorney talked, I talked,
the seller did more begging, but it didn't make any
difference—the insurance company refused to
yield. I couldn't understand their position. This was
an opportunity for them to get rid of the present
owners—with whom they had been unhappy—and
secure a very substantial company on the mortgage.
Finally, I realized what they were angling for:
Blood!

Next time you pass one of those insurance
company skyscrapers, look closely between the
bricks. You probably thought they were held together by cement. Not so. That substance between
the bricks is dried, human blood. All of those
friendly insurance companies—the ones who run
the ads on television showing their agents helping

out some nice neighborhood family—have built their buildings on human blood.

Apparently they were getting ready to build a new building, because the upshot of our meeting was that the seller would have to give a couple of pints in order to induce the insurance company to allow the sale to go through. Finally—after considerably more begging, tears and hard luck stories—the working partner voluntarily allowed the insurance company to stick the needle in his arm and "reluctantly" extract a "mortgage transfer fee."

After we left the insurance company, the working partner, though bitter about what the insurance company had done to him, was elated nearly to the point of tears over the fact that the sale was apparently going to close. He told me and my attorney that he was sincerely grateful to us and would never forget what we had done for him by going to Cincinnati and helping to convince the insurance company to agree to the transfer of the property.

I then stepped inside a phone booth and changed into a hare costume which I happened to have in my briefcase, thus enabling my masochistic thought processes to come up with the following brilliant line of reasoning: since everything seemed to be under control now, and since I didn't want anything to get in the way of the hot romance that was going on between the working partner and me, I told my attorney (blush) that he need not accompany us to the closing.

So off to Dayton I went, with my thankful pal—

"Hold up on the praise, Sweetheart, till I finish dressing."

the working partner—smothering me with praise all along the way.

This time I was the one who went under the ether; and when I did, the last thing I remembered was waiting around in the attorney's reception room, sucking my thumb and playing with my yo-yo while the closing was taking place in another room. The working partner came bustling out of the closing room and announced that everything was "all set," then said that we were all going out to dinner and celebrate. I asked him about my commission, but he told me not to worry about it; he said that he was "taking care of everything." He seemed so jubilant that I hated to do anything to dampen his spirits.

All parties to the closing attended the celebration dinner, including the Washington partner who had refused to sign my commission agreement. (As I had counted on from the beginning, he had signed all of the documents necessary to close the deal, which of and by itself legally indicated that he approved of the sale.)

Even at the celebration dinner the working partner continued to heap praise on me in front of everyone. I was so flattered that I was tempted to pull out my yo-yo and show them a couple of new tricks I'd learned while they had been busy closing the sale. But when I saw that the first course being served was turtle soup, I began to come out of my sedation; it was wonderful being invited to dinner, but not when I realized that I was on the menu. I quickly reminded myself of my past experiences, my

"Everything's all set. Let's go celebrate."

philosophy and my techniques, and remembered that I had been dealing with an extreme Type Number One who had made it clear to me that the name of the game was to get as many chips as you could by whatever means necessary. I decided that I had to find a way to talk to the working partner as soon as possible.

After about an hour, the working partner got up to go to the men's room, so I also excused myself. It wasn't exactly my idea of the best place to conduct business, but I had already shed my hare costume, and, as a true tortoise once again, I trudged ahead even under those awkward circumstances. There in the men's room I told the working partner that I didn't want to ruin his celebration, but that I had not yet received my commission as promised.

Then came the classic **Dayton Men's Room Address:**

The Type Number One working partner smiled, put his arm around my shoulder, and said, "Listen, the buyer's holding up some of the funds for a few months pending my performance of certain conditions in the sale agreement. On top of that, the insurance company hit me with the transfer fee this morning (remember, it was *I* who had saved him with the insurance company), so there isn't a dime left to give you today. But as soon as we work out the other items, I'll have enough to pay you." He then looked me right in the eye—as his smile broadened into a toothy grin very reminiscent of the Big Bad Wolf—and said, "Don't worry, I'll take care of you (cackle, cackle)."

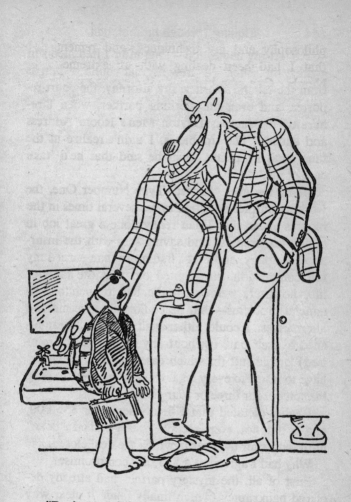

"Don't worry, I'll take care of you (cackle, cackle)."

P.S. At my deposition—long after I had filed suit against the sellers—I drew a great round of laughs from the sellers' attorney, my attorney, the court reporter, and even the working partner, when I reiterated the famous Dayton Men's Room Address and added: "The trouble is, I didn't realize at the time what he meant when he said that he'd 'take care of me.'"

Being the ever "honest" Type Number One, the working partner admitted to me several times in the months ahead that I had really done a great job in selling his property and saving him with the insurance company, and that I had more than earned my full commission. He pointed out that the facts of life, however, were such—he had tremendous financial problems—that he could only give me two alternatives: I could either wait until he "straightened himself out" (without any specific date promised) or file suit (in which case, he said, he would have to resort to every legal trick in the book to drag the suit out for three or four years).

Reality dictated that I finally settle for $35,000, and I did not even receive that glorified "bone" until long after the year in which the deal closed.

Why had I agreed to a $35,000 compromise?

First of all, the mystery partner had already declared bankruptcy (which finally made it clear why he was such a mystery), and thus I had no recourse against him. Secondly, it turned out that there was a clause in the limited partnership agreement which —contrary to what the working partner had assured me of—specifically *prevented* him from entering into a contract for the sale of the Dayton property without the approval of the Washington partner. (And my intuition told me that all three partners would, of course, stick by the rules of the jungle and thus offer up The Big Lie—in this case, the "fact" that I was notified of the existence of the sale prevention clause prior to my going ahead and working on the deal—when called upon to testify.) In addition, the Washington partner pointed out that he had specifically refused to sign the contract when I visited him in Washington, and this gave his personal position at least some degree of credibility even though his statement—from a pure legal standpoint—was meaningless.

My commission agreements were written in such a way that whoever signed them always signed personally—not as a partner in a partnership or as an officer in a corporation. Therefore, about the only hope I had left was to go after the working partner, and I didn't like the prospects of collecting from him. Indications were that he'd been in financial difficulty for quite some time, and from all I could gather, things were getting perhaps worse rather than better. If the suit dragged on much longer, I had to recognize the distinct possibility of his going broke in the meantime; I might then spend a lot of added time, energy and money, and still not collect a penny.

The result was that I grabbed what I could—which was $35,000—and called it a day. Shame on me: I had a tremendous image, I had all of the necessary legal tools, and I had executed above and beyond the call of duty; and in addition I had also recognized very early in the game that I was dealing with an extreme Type Number One, so I certainly felt like I was prepared. But when it came to the showdown—when I reached the one yard line—I relaxed just enough to commit an infraction on the touchdown play.

My attorney never asked me how I felt after the Dayton closing, but if he had, I would undoubtedly have replied: "Dumb."

Chapter 18

The Tortoise Returns
To True Form

Translation: *By doing the right thing instead of the instinctive thing, I survived a couple of tricky Type Number Twos.*

I went into my Memphis deal determined never again to be lulled into a mental lapse. The Dayton fiasco had reminded me that I must move swiftly at the first sign of trouble.

In Memphis—right from the outset—I was hoping for the best but expecting the worst with regard to receiving my commission if a sale were concluded. I was wary because my trained eye had immediately spotted the two main partners as Type

Number Twos, and, as I've already pointed out, Type Number Twos are the most devious, deceitful and treacherous of the three types of people in the business world.

One of the partners—who also happened to be an attorney—was what I would describe as an over-obvious Type Number Two. He was one of those back-slapping type of guys, always laughing and joking and telling you what a "good ol' boy" you were—a "wheeler-dealer" attorney who was in no way related to the "normal," run-of-the-mill deal-killer type. Wheeler-dealer attorneys either don't practice law at all or practice it only as a sideline, using their law certificates as respectable fronts for digging up good business deals and making the most of them. I don't say this facetiously or deroga-torily, because I actually consider it to be a clever marketing approach. (In fact, if I had it to do over again, and if college—other than Screw U.—did not get in the way of learning, I think I'd go through law school just to be able to use the marketing approach of being an attorney.)

The other partner was a different kind of Type Number Two—a sort of "mumbler." He was nei-ther nice like a Type Number Three, nor direct like a Type Number One; it was therefore very easy to label him.

What with being constantly slapped on the back and told that I was a "good ol' boy" by the wheeler-dealer attorney partner, and being mumbled at by the other partner, I had all I could do to protect my flanks. Naturally I was licensed as a real estate broker in Tennessee, had a signed commission agreement with the sellers, and had made sure that the usual amount of certified mail went back and forth between my office and the principals, so I was certainly in a strong legal position. I also had the usual image factors going for me, including my flitting in and out of Memphis via the Learjet.

Our original commission agreement called for a purchase price of about $1.2 million over a combined first mortgage balance of approximately $3.6 million, or a total purchase price in excess of $4.8 million.

About a month after we signed the commission agreement, the buyer of my Dayton deal sent a written offer of $950,000 (over the mortgages) for the two apartment developments. He came to Memphis and made a personal inspection of the properties, at which time the sellers informed him that a $950,000 offering price was too low. With that, my buyer departed Memphis and the situation was left hanging in the air.

In the meantime, the party who had purchased the Kansas City properties made an offer of $1.4 million (over the mortgages) for the Memphis apartments, but it was not an all cash offer. Trooping back to Memphis with this buyer, I succeeded in getting Mumbles and Good Ol' Boy to sign a tentative agreement to sell at the $1.4 million figure. However, after the buyer and I left Memphis, my Type Number Two pals continued to fiddle around while both the $1.4 million offer and the $950,000 offer burned.

Incredibly, about a month later I was able to come up with still a third prospective buyer (the third "buyer" actually consisted of several partners) for the property, this time from the Pittsburgh area. One of the partners traveled to Memphis to meet Tennessee's answer to Laurel and Hardy, and after many hours of discussions and negotiations, he went back home to discuss the deal with his associates. Another one of the Pittsburgh partners then came to Memphis and submitted a purchase contract that called for $1.075 million over the mortgages; however, it had a number of unreasonable strings attached to it, so Mumbles and Good Ol' Boy turned it down. About a week after that, the Pittsburgh buyers upped their offer to $1.275 million, but the terms of that offer were even more unreasonable than the first one.

Following the last Pittsburgh offer, my Dayton buyer then stepped back into the bidding and raised his offer to $1 million—with the condition that it be accepted within twenty days. And with still further resistance from Memphis, the Dayton buyer increased his bid yet again—to $1.1 million—but $200,000 of the purchase price was to be in the form of a ten-year "purchase money mortgage" at the rate of 6% per annum.

After a few more weeks of fiddling around, Mumbles and Good Ol' Boy managed to play all three hands against each other so well that Memphis just about burned down around them, and consequently they lost all three deals. This was quite painful for me because my experience had been that if I were lucky enough to find just one buyer who was serious enough to make a personal inspection and submit a written offer on a given property, I was in great shape. I was really disgusted over the fact that in this particular deal I had produced not one, not two, but three serious buyers—buyers who had been interested enough to make personal inspections of the properties and submit written offers —yet still had not made a sale. Even though the Memphis deal looked very makable on the surface, I was pretty convinced that the sellers, for some reason, were intent on fiddling around until the projects went bankrupt. I was about ready to write off the whole thing as just another bad experience.

Before doing so, however, I figured that I may as well present the deal to a few more prospective buyers. And, hard as it was for me to believe, I came up with yet another serious purchaser, this one from Cleveland. Like the three previous buyers, the fourth one indicated that he was prepared to make a trip to Memphis. I told myself that I was a glutton for punishment and that I should not get sucked into wasting the time and expense of making a fourth trip. I was really convinced that the sellers were crazy and were just getting some sort of perverted thrill out of having people pursue the purchase of their properties. As you might suspect, however, the tortoise within me won out, and back to Memphis I went.

At that point it started to become obvious that

the sellers were in serious financial trouble. In fact they made a special trip to New York in an attempt to revive one of my previous offers. In what looked like a state of panic, Mumbles sent me a telegram from New York saying that he and his partner would accept the $1.1 million verbal offer the Cleveland buyer had made, but only on two conditions.

The first was that I had to agree to cut my commission to $50,000. The second was that the buyer would have to officially acknowledge the $1.1 million offer by noon the next day. But as I said earlier, you don't bluff wealthy people; they have staying power. My buyers, of course, refused to be hurried into the acknowledgement, and the deal was off.

A few days later I received another telegram from Mumbles (who was still wandering through the streets of New York trying to put a deal together) informing me that he and Good Ol' Boy were unilaterally canceling our commission agreement and that all deals we had talked about were officially off. I thought it was a rather ridiculous action on their part since I had produced no less than four legitimate, serious prospective purchasers for their properties.

In the meantime I was able to get my Cleveland buyer to make his $1.1 million offer official, so I had another major decision to make: Should I stop throwing good money after bad, or was my investment in Memphis already so big that I couldn't afford to stop trying to put a deal together? I decided to try just one more time, but promised myself—

come hell or high water—that this would be the last trip I'd make to the land of Mumbles and Good Ol' Boy.

I explained to my now extremely panicked Type Number Two Memphis friends that my buyer was very serious about going through with a quick closing on the properties at the $1.1 million figure. And that's when Mumbles told me, in no uncertain terms, that my commission had actually been at the root of blowing up each of the other deals and that there was no way I could expect to make a $140,000 fee unless I was able to get the offering price up to the original $1.2 million+ asking price. Talking very clearly for the first time, Mumbles let me know that even though he was impressed with my Learjet, he had no desire to help pay for it.

I had to make a decision. I had already made an incredible six trips to Memphis—including four trips with serious buyers—and had produced four written offers. In each of the first three cases the dynamic duo from Memphis had fiddled around until the offer slipped away. Now I knew that the fourth one was also about to be lost if something didn't happen pretty quick. I knew there was no way that I was ever going to get lured back into making another trip to Memphis, or even submitting the property to another prospective buyer, if the Cleveland offer didn't close. I therefore considered the deal to be a lost cause and rationalized that if I could make anything at all, I would look upon it as just a lucky bonus.

After several hours of negotiations, I finally

agreed to a commission of $75,000 on a sale price of $1.1 million. We drew up a new commission agreement similar to the first one, except for a clause which stated that the Memphis sellers agreed to accept a price of $1.1 million from the Cleveland buyer and that they would pay me a $75,000 commission if the deal was finalized.

The Cleveland buyer subsequently put his $1.1 million offer in writing and we immediately began working toward a closing.

But as we neared the closing, both my attorney and I began to have difficulty getting either of the sellers on the telephone—a sure sign of trouble. Finally, on the Friday before the first closing (the sale was to take place in two stages since the second property was not yet completed), my attorney and I managed to get Good Ol' Boy on the phone.

He was his old jovial self—darn near slapping me on the back right through the telephone—and indicated that "as far as he knew, everything was all set." He said he didn't foresee any problems with my commission, and even reassured us that we were still "good ol' boys" in his eyes. (At that advanced stage of learning, I interpreted his statement to mean that I would soon be the victim of a commissiondectomy if I didn't move fast.)

I felt that my posture contained a slight puncture in this particular deal, so I tried a new twist. Since one of the sellers (Good Ol' Boy) was an attorney, and since my own attorney had already had several discussions with both Good Ol' Boy and the sellers' attorney, I thought perhaps it would be a good idea to totally rely on the unwritten Universal Attorney-to-Attorney Respect Law. I "called an audible at the line" and sent my attorney to the Memphis closing alone, figuring that in this one situation it was I who was the weak link.

At the closing, my attorney presented a copy of the signed commission agreement to both the sellers' attorney and the title company handling the proceedings. The sellers' attorney then asked my lawyer to kindly wait in the reception room (another sure sign of trouble) while the buyer and sellers "talked." Believe it or not, the parties then proceeded to close the sale in my attorney's absence.

The buyer had tried to cooperate with me in every way possible, but had taken the usual ostrich position that the matter of my commission was between the sellers and me. He did insist that my name be inserted in the purchase contract as the broker of record, but since that agreement also stated that it was the sellers' responsibility to pay my commission, the buyer had probably assumed it would be paid right after the closing.

Unfortunately, he was wrong, and this time it was my attorney who got caught sucking his thumb and playing with his yo-yo in the reception room while the real game was being played behind closed doors. Another new curve had been thrown at me in the jungle: I had never considered the possibility of Legalman faking me out by allowing a closing to occur on the one hand, and at the same time being a party to a plot to blatantly deceive a fellow attorney.

The unwritten Universal Attorney-to-Attorney Respect Law had failed for the first time. After I heard about it, I just shook my head and thought to myself that maybe someday I would realize that the number of ways a seller can think of to do a broker out of his chips is infinite.

To top everything off, the day after the closing I received a certified letter from the sellers' lawyer saying that the commission agreement was terminated for "breach" on my part, and that it was completely null and void. It was obviously an absurd letter, but it was quite a learning experience. The letter was dated the day after Good Ol' Boy had assured my attorney and me over the phone that "everything was all set." It was postmarked on Sunday (one day after it was written), making it obvious that the sellers had intended for it to arrive subsequent to the closing (which was scheduled to take place on Monday).

In other words, while Good Ol' Boy was telling my lawyer over the phone that he "didn't foresee any problems with my commission," he and Mumbles were already planning to send me a letter claiming that I wasn't entitled to any commission at all. Then at the closing, the sellers and their attorney had actually tricked my attorney out of the room and hurried through the proceedings before he realized what was going on.

I had been through some pretty crummy situations before—both during and after my days at Screw U.—but I had never seen anything quite like this. For overall Type Number Two treachery, it's true that no one ever quite measured up to my St. Louis seller. But for sheer diabolical plotting, deception and all-out effort, I had never conceived of anything like what took place in Memphis. I wasn't shocked that the principals were trying to cheat me out of my commission, just awed by the extent to which they were willing to go to try to out-maneuver me in an effort to offset the legal tools I possessed.

My attorney took the matter personally since the unwritten Universal Attorney-to-Attorney Respect Law had been violated. He sent the sellers' attorney a letter in which he stated, among other things, that his (the sellers' attorney's) letter was unfounded and ridiculous, that it was too late, that he should not have been communicating directly with another attorney's client, and that if he (my attorney) had ever treated another attorney the way he (the sellers' attorney) and Good Ol' Boy had treated him (my attorney), he (my attorney) would expect to be up before the bar association.

But the game did not end there.

Fortunately, the smaller of the two properties had yet to be closed because construction and occupancy requirements were not yet completed. My attorney and I were lucky enough to find a brilliant young trial lawyer in Memphis to take my case, and I must say that had it not been for his aggressiveness and quick action I might never have seen a dime. He managed to get an attachment against the owners and the property involved in the second closing, although I had to put up a bond to help accomplish it. Unlike Dayton, I had moved swiftly and, with some good fortune, had managed to avert a total catastrophe. I was able to do this only because I had those three great legal tools in my bag—real estate license, commission agreement and certified mail—and had not allowed myself to become lax.

In addition to suing the two sellers, I also sued the title company. About a week after the suit was filed, I wrote a letter to the president of the title company, telling him that I thought it was incredible that an institution the size of his firm would be a party to such deception. I again put him on notice about the commission agreement that existed between the sellers and me, and enclosed another copy of it. I also said that I was holding him personally responsible for seeing to it that my commission was paid at the second closing. Incredibly, though, my commission was not paid at that closing, either (although the court did hold up the proceeds of the sale).

Shortly after the year in which I closed the deal, the sellers—undoubtedly out of financial desperation—made a $50,000 settlement offer. My Memphis attorney encouraged me not to be in any hurry to accept the offer—and I probably should have listened to him—but the day before the first depositions were to be taken, I accepted it.

Once again I had examined the downside closely; it was more than just a matter of principle. The sellers—like so many other sellers with whom I had dealt—were in shaky financial condition, and I had to consider the possibility of their going broke; in that event I probably wouldn't be able to collect anything at all. Also, there was the usual advantage for the side in the wrong: the case could take several years to go through the courts while I expended thousands of dollars in legal fees, travel expenses and other costs. As a result, even if I won I would probably be lucky to come out with a net of $50,000.

This is a good example of why I emphasized that the main purpose of real estate licenses, brokerage agreements and certified mail is to *avoid* having legal problems—to avoid lawsuits. If the guy you're dealing with decides to crash your "civil defense" even when he knows that you have all of the legal tools on your side, the reality is that you'll probably still be a loser if you have to go the whole route and win it through the courts; you either win in the jungle or you don't win at all.

The Memphis deal reaffirmed the fact that sellers —particularly Type Number Twos—will go to absolutely any extreme to avoid paying commissions. In addition, it once again reminded me that banks, title companies and other "great American institutions" have built their corporate empires on human blood, and that I should not get lulled into a false sense of security just because they happened to be involved in any given deal. Finally, it put me on guard to the fact that just because a guy happened to be an attorney, that didn't mean he was above being a party to a devious plot to do me out of my commission. This was certainly an unusual role for Legalman—he normally just plays a good clean game of hard-nosed defense—but it was another new jungle danger to watch for in the future.

All in all, though, I was somewhat satisfied with the outcome in Memphis. I had spotted Good Ol' Boy and Mumbles as Type Number Twos from the very beginning and had just played along with their act. I had also not only secured all of the necessary legal tools, but—as was not the case in Dayton—once I saw the sellers swinging their axe, I had taken swift action.

True, the sellers had managed to nip off the ends of a couple of my fingers, but at least I had been quick enough to walk away with sufficient chips to be able to afford a new paint job on my badly scarred shell.

Chapter 19

Insuring Myself Against Penalties

Translation: *The buyer's full support made my getting paid a near certainty.*

My Dallas closing—the sale of two apartment developments totaling approximately 340 units—served as a model for applying my philosophy to a specific objective through the use of specific techniques. It was quick, it was smooth, and there were no last minute anxieties.

There were two factors, in particular, which were very significant in this deal:

The first was that I used my strong posture—which I had initially achieved through image building—to get the seller to sign a commission agreement based on 5½% of the total selling price rath-

er than the normal 3% figure I usually used. Since
my commission had been knocked down in both
Dayton and Memphis, and since reducing my commission was, I felt, the very least that any seller
would try to do to me, I thought it would be interesting to see the psychological effects of using a
higher commission percentage in my agreement;
then when the usual commissiondectomy attempt
began, I could always afford to cut the commission
down, knowing that my real aim—from the beginning—was only to receive something in the area of
3%.

I had developed a good rapport with the seller—
who lived in San Antonio, although his apartment
projects were in Dallas—with my image being
strong from the very beginning. And by shuffling
him back and forth between Dallas and San Antonio on my Learjet, I only continued to improve it. I
was in awe of the effects of the principle of intimidation: just a year earlier I probably would not have
been able to get this seller to even sign a commission
agreement because my posture was weak; now with
the Earth brochure, the Learjet, and the addition of
one other big image factor—a track record of having closed several major deals—I was not only able
to get the seller to sign an agreement, but sign one
that called for a commission percentage nearly dou-
ble that of most of my previous agreements (and
about 25 times greater than the percentage of the
sale price my St. Louis "bone" had figured out to
be). I really felt that the Theory of Intimidation was
now in high gear. I could clearly see the results—

the proof that it was not what I was saying and
doing that made the difference, but what my posture was when I was saying and doing it.

Since the original contract indicated an asking
price of nearly $3 million, my commission "going
in" was almost $150,000; but in my own mind I
knew that what I was actually shooting for was a
commission in the area of only $90,000 (based on
3% of the asking price). Furthermore, I knew that if
I were fortunate enough to achieve a closing, the
final selling price—as with all sales—would be considerably below the original asking price.

Sure enough, when money finally changed hands
the price was closer to $2.7 million than $3 million
(technically it was less than $1.7 million because
the buyer actually purchased only a one-half interest in the properties). My final gross commission
was $100,000 (nearly 4% of the final purchase
price and over 6% of the "technical" purchase
price). Thus by starting out with an unusually high
commission rate, I was able to walk away with at
least $20,000 more than I might have ordinarily re-
ceived under my normal 3% formula.

The second significant ingredient in the Dallas
closing was that I had an "insurance policy" against
not getting paid. As usual, in addition to my commission agreement I possessed the other two legal
tools: a brokerage license in the state of Texas and
an excessive amount of certified mail going from me
to the principals. But, more important, I also had a
buyer who was willing to step over the line and

make my getting paid one of the conditions of the closing.

There were many reasons why I had this support, but I believe the most important one was the fact that the buyer was smart enough—and had sufficient foresight—to understand that it was to his advantage to see to it that I was treated fairly. Even though I had never completed a sale with this particular purchaser, I had submitted many write-ups to him, and being a major buyer of properties he had enough experience to recognize the fact that I did my job well; my presentations were good and I was prompt and aggressive in following up on his initial interest in properties. In other words, I had "execution power" with him. In addition to everything else, it didn't hurt to have my Earth brochure, the Learjet, and a track record of having recently completed several major sales—components of "image power." Thinking long-range, he probably considered it to be in his best interest for me to receive my commission.

I would have to say that this was an ideal situation. It reminded me very much of the association I had had with my elderly Type Number One professor at Screw U., when I was brokering second mortgages just a couple of years earlier. This factor was so powerful that it could even make up for a lack of legal tools; on the other hand, the fact that I did have the three legal tools going for me made the addition of the full support of the buyer work like a fail-safe insurance policy.

Talk about a complete reversal of form: I had advanced 180 degrees to the other extreme from where I'd been a few years earlier. With the support of the buyer, plus all of my posture factors, I had every exit covered. The seller had no way to turn and as a result he did not even infer the possibility of a commissiondectomy. This was civil defense at its best. In fact, things went so smoothly that I was never even sure whether the seller was a Type Number One or Type Number Two. And it really didn't matter; it simply was not a factor in this transaction. By gaining the full support of the buyer, I had removed temptation from the seller's grasp.

And since the seller seemed to be in the usual financial bind, we were also able to get good cooperation from Legalman. This, coupled with the fact that I had the buyer's full support, made the last yard a breeze. As a result, the closing went very smoothly; in fact, from an overall standpoint it was by far the quickest deal I ever closed (less than three months elapsed between the time my commission agreement was signed and the closing).

Even though it was obvious that I had the buyer's support, I brought my attorney along to the closing. The buyer assured me that this wasn't necessary, but I was glad I did because it also gave my attorney the opportunity to become good friends with the buyer—and that made future dealings even easier to handle. After all the papers had been signed and the closing was, for all practical purposes, wrapped up (even though the sale was technically closed, there were a couple of formalities to be taken care of the next morning), I left Dallas to attend to another deal while my attorney stayed behind to collect my fee.

When my attorney remitted the commission to me, he enclosed a letter in which he pointed out that because of some of the usual last minute contingencies, the buyer's attorney had wanted to escrow $100,000 from the seller's proceeds and $25,000 from my commission; the buyer, however, had insisted that none of my money be held back. He closed the letter by saying, ". . . which indicates to me that he (the buyer) certainly thinks a good deal of you." That sentence summed it up in a nutshell. Although I couldn't count on having this kind of insurance policy in the future, I felt, at the time, that I had reached the optimum posture—total credibility—a real estate broker could hope to attain.

Not very exciting to write about, but I wish that my three previous closings, as well as the scores of deals which did not close, had been this "unexciting;" I had pulled $100,000 worth of chips off the table without even getting so much as a manicure.

There was no longer the slightest doubt in my mind that intimidation was the key to winning.

Chapter 20

Sticking With A Winning Formula

Translation: *My second deal in a row with the buyer's full support.*

Even though I wasn't able to negotiate an agreement with a higher than usual commission rate, I managed to retain the other key Dallas ingredient—"buyer insurance"—in my Omaha closing; the same buyer who had purchased the Dallas apartments also bought my Omaha properties.

In addition to having the buyer's support, there were three other things I considered to be significant in the Omaha deal:

First was the fact that it was an extremely complicated sale in that it involved 15 properties, and the final structuring of the sale was a purchase of a one-half interest in the apartment developments on a sale-leaseback basis (the same formula which had been used in Dallas). Since the buyer couldn't come anywhere near the asking price of close to $2.7 million over the mortgages, we structured a sale that called for his company to purchase a 50% interest in the 15 properties for $1.3 million, then lease its half back to the seller. My job was to get the owner to understand the advantages of such a sale, which fortunately I was able to do.

The second significant factor in Omaha was that even though the sale price was technically only about one-half of the original asking price, and even though my commission agreement called for only 3% of the total selling price, I was able to get paid on the basis of a 100% sale rather than the actual 50% sale that was concluded. Since the owner technically sold only a one-half interest in his 15 properties, the real selling price was in the area of $4.5 million, rather than the $9 million+ asking price stated in my commission agreement. The seller could have "legally" argued that my commission should only be 3% of approximately $4.5 million, or about $135,000. But because of my strong posture—and particularly because of the full support of the buyer—I was able to hold out for a gross commission of $238,000.

I considered this to be an even greater accomplishment than the Dallas sale because I didn't have the advantage of starting out with a 5½% commission rate in my brokerage agreement. I had started out at only 3%, so based on my own wording in the agreement I was not "entitled" to more than about $135,000. But by having completely reversed the roles of the intimidator and intimidatee, I was able to perform what you might call a "reverse-commis-siondectomy"—I actually succeeded in *increasing* my commission over and above what it appeared it should have been according to the commission agreement.

My reason for insisting that my commission be based on a full sale was that everyone involved knew that the sale of a one-half interest was merely a way of structuring the deal. In truth I had done the same amount of work as if the deal had closed on a normal 100% sale basis, so I saw no reason why I should be penalized. Further, there were various stipulations in the purchase agreement whereby the buyer could either end up owning the other halves of the properties through default or could purchase them at a very low price. It therefore might have been only a matter of a short period of time until the buyer ended up owning 100% of the properties (and sure enough, that's exactly what did happen).

The third significant ingredient in Omaha was that I ran into a new variety of Type Number Two. As you might have observed by now, more people fall into the Type Number Two category than any other. This is because very few people have the guts or inherent "honesty" to be Type Number Ones, and there aren't many people with any degree of success who are stupid enough to be Type Number Threes.

When you categorize people into just three groups, you obviously have numerous subtle variations within each group. For example, you'll remember that one of the Type Number Twos in my Memphis deal had been a back-slapping, "good ol' boy" variation and the other had been a "mumbler."

In the case of Omaha, the seller was a "dumb-as-a-fox" Type Number Two. He was a huge man—I would estimate at least 240 pounds—and came across as a very docile, "nice" guy, always looking confused and scratching his head. People who look confused and scratch their heads tend to relax the opposition; they do not pose a visible threat (a very good selling technique, I might add).

But this seller had still another "marketing tool" going for him: not only was he big and not only did he appear to be docile and confused, but he also spoke with a rather thick European accent. For some reason—perhaps it's American presumptuousness—people often make the mistake of assuming that persons with foreign accents don't know what's going on. Obviously this is ridiculous. The fact remains, however, that a European accent, as a general rule, does seem to instinctively lull people into a state of relaxation. Later I was to find that the Omaha seller was, in fact, one of the most cunning and clever people I would meet in the real estate business. From that standpoint, it was a very educational experience for me, and one in which I was again able to earn while I learned.

After signing up the deal, I left two of my secretaries behind in Omaha to gather up the tremendous amount of material needed to do presentations on 15 properties. It wasn't until a month or so after this that I registered the eventual buyer—the man who had shown full support for me in my Dallas closing—with the Omaha owner. Shortly thereafter, I flew to Milwaukee to pick up the buyer and we cruised down to Omaha in the Learjet for one of those thrilling episodes of brick-staring.

Fortunately it was summer, so Omaha was still accessible to aircraft. If you aren't too familiar with Nebraska, I should point out that the seasons of the year are very important when it comes to doing business there. Nebraska has its own special Ice Age, and it takes place every year between fall and spring when the state is covered by a glacier. Taking advantage of the temporary absence of the glacial covering, I suggested that the buyer, the seller and I jump into my Learjet and view the 15 properties from the air.

If you've never been inside a Learjet, there's no way you can appreciate how lousy my suggestion turned out to be. The inside of a Learjet is about the size of a coffin; if you're over ten years of age, you can't stand up in that aircraft. About the only movement it was intended to allow for is scratching your ear.

But there we were, buzzing over Omaha at an altitude of just a few hundred feet, with this massive 240-pound seller hurling himself from one side of the plane to the other and shouting, in a thick European accent, that we were just coming over . . . no,

"Duh . . . vee jus paz over annuder vun of mine propurtees."

we were just going over . . . no, we had just *passed* over another of his properties. Just about the time the buyer or I would be getting to the window out of which the seller was pointing, Europe's answer to Brer Bear would be lunging to the other side of the plane, usually resulting in a "shall we dance" type of collision situation on our knees. I darn near cracked my shell getting slammed around between the seller and the sides of the flying coffin.

Bruised and battered, the buyer and I repeated the tour of the 15 properties on the ground, although that turned out to be an even worse experience. The owner drove us from project to project in his car, seemingly without much of a decrease in speed from that which we had experienced in my Learjet.

After the normal hassling back and forth—including a courageous goal line stand by Legalman—we managed to get the deal closed on the 50% sale-leaseback basis. Having had proof in Dallas that I had the full support of the buyer, I used my valuable time to work on other deals; I did not even attend the closing—I had my attorney collect the $238,000 commission for me.

I could not help recalling how just a few years earlier I had startled everyone in that first deal in Cincinnati by showing up at the closing with my own attorney. Now, working from a posture of absolute strength—imagewise, legalwise and executionwise—and having the full support of the buyer, it was not only taken for granted that my attorney would be at the closing, but it was not even necessary for me to take the time to make a personal appearance myself.

Omaha was the last deal I closed during the first twelve-month period in which I put my new philosophy into effect. And I must say that it was a perfect note on which to end the year's work. By this time the Earth brochure, the Learjet, and a track record of many major closings—in addition to all of the other factors I had going for me—had become my accepted trademarks. Groveling around on my hands and knees for "bones" now seemed like a distant nightmare. In Omaha I had again proven to myself, beyond a shadow of a doubt, that it isn't what a person says or does that counts, but what his posture is when he says or does it.

Understanding the reality of the Theory of Intimidation had led to the ultimate in real estate selling: the performance of a "reverse-commissiondectomy."

Chapter 21

Why Had The Tortoise Been Able To Hit The Jackpot?

Translation: *What was behind my winning through intimidation?*

Displayed in this chapter is a summary chart of the six deals I've just described. All of these properties were sold by me during the very first year following the organization and implementation of my philosophy and techniques. But it's important to remember that these fat five- and six-figure commissions represent only a small fraction of the total number of deals I worked on during that year.

Without the Theory of Sustenance of a Positive Attitude Through the Assumption of a Negative

Result, there is no possible way that I could have ever received any one of these commissions. The disappointment and frustration I endured in working on the scores upon scores of deals that did not close, or for which I did not get paid, would have completely discouraged me had it not been for my understanding of the reality that *most deals simply do not close because of factors beyond the salesman's control.*

(And that latter statement, my friends, is reality —not the way you or I *wish* things to be, but the way they really *are;* either you acknowledge that fact and use it to your benefit or it will automatically work against you.)

When I had organized my philosophy and techniques, my hopes for success basically rested upon the Theory of Reality. It was the very foundation— the backbone—for the rest of my philosophy. Without this theory, all of my other theories combined— including the Theory of Intimidation—could not have given me the results I obtained. And certainly any techniques for applying my philosophy would have been meaningless.

In order to take the proper action regarding anything, you first have to be sure of what that "thing" is. Having the greatest cure in the world for the common cold doesn't help a heck of a lot if the ailment you're treating is the mumps.

It was my unwavering determination to face reality—to recognize and acknowledge it even though it was hard to swallow at times—that served as my foundation. It was only after I felt confident that I

City	Description of Real Estate	Approximate Sale Price	Actual Gross Commission Received
Kansas City #1	4 apartment developments	$ 6,500,000	$221,446.50
Kansas City #2	4 apartment developments	6,000,000	205,454.89
Dayton	apartment development	4,000,000	35,000.00
Memphis	2 apartment developments	4,500,000	50,000.00
Dallas	2 apartment developments	1,600,000*	100,000.00
Omaha	15 apartment developments	4,500,000*	238,000.00
		$27,100,000	$849,901.39

*The actual values of the Dallas and Omaha properties were closer to $2,700,000 and $7,700,000, respectively, but I used only one-half of the mortgage balances in calculating the sales prices because the buyer originally purchased only a one-half interest in these two properties. Based on the higher values, the approximate total of the sales prices of all the properties involved in the six closings was closer to $31,400,000.

knew what the "thing" was ("reality isn't the way you wish things to be, nor the way they appear to be, but the way they actually are") that I was prepared to take proper action. Only then did my study and analysis of the facts (my real-life experiences) lead to the structuring of my philosophy and a method (my techniques) for using reality to my benefit rather than allowing it to work against me.

Because my philosophy was based on reality, all of my techniques were either directly or indirectly aimed at the most important reality of all: the necessity of getting paid. It was reality that had led me to this "fifth step" of what I had always heard described as "the four steps of selling."

Regardless of the "product" or "service," selling is not an end in itself; selling is only a means to an end: receiving "income." Contrary to the emphasis in many "success" and "how to" books, closing deals is not the name of the game; it is only a means to the end of walking away with chips in your hand. Reality dictates that the mere closing of deals will not pay your grocery bills; only getting paid will do that. In business, love, and life in general, "getting paid" is what it's all about.

I, like most people I've known, often hid my eyes from the realities of the jungle because they seemed too "brutal" to accept. But whether or not I accepted them did not change the fact that they were realities. It wasn't until I finally forced myself to stop being an ostrich that I was able to start making some headway in the jungle. "Brutal" is another one of those freely used, relative words. Relative to the candyland rules of goody-two-shoesism taught in so many "success" books, the realities of the jungle may seem "brutal;" but relative to the fantasies which actually support those rules, the realities of the jungle are comforting.

Based on my interpretations of reality and relativity, the techniques I used were not "brutal," either. I merely fought fire with fire: the techniques were no more brutal than the realities they were intended to reckon with. And realities are nothing more than "things"—not "good" or "bad," not "brutal" or "comforting"—they just *are*.

Because of this I have to admit that when I look back on characters like my Type Number Three professor in my first deal in Cincinnati, the Big Bad Wolf in Dayton, Mumbles and Good Ol' Boy in Memphis, or Brer Bear in Omaha, a warm feeling of nostalgia comes over me. What the heck—they were just playing the game to win.

So you get a little banged up now and then . . . so what? I believe in the Ice Ball Theory: business is just a game and life is only a bigger game. And when you're playing a game, it's amateurish to dislike your opponent just because he wins. With everything in proper perspective, I have to admire all of those Type Number Ones, Twos and Threes who made so many good plays against me. All they were doing was trying to win by the rules of the game; it's just that the game happens to be played in a jungle, and thus the rules of the jungle prevail.

On the other hand, just because you admire an opponent's ability certainly doesn't mean that you should *help* him to get more chips. He'd like you to help him, but, believe me, he doesn't expect it. Like him, you should do what's in *your* best interest. Reality is such that it simply isn't true that if you do a good job, you'll get what you deserve. That kind of attitude will only turn you into a cobweb-covered skeleton with a pile of cigar butts where your chips should be. And remember: looking out for your best interest does not conflict with your doing a good job at whatever it is that you're supposed to get paid for; it simply means that you make sure you *do* get paid for the good service you render. You have the right to be remunerated for a good performance, and don't allow *anyone* to intimidate you into thinking otherwise.

Nor do you have to feel contempt for someone like Legalman. You must understand that he is not out to get *you* when he kills your deal. If there is one thing he's not, it's particular; he doesn't discriminate when it comes to killing deals. He's just doing his thing. By all means, try like the devil to win, but if Legalman stops you on downs on the one yard line, give him his proper credit; don't be afraid to admire him for displaying a valiant goal line stand.

In closing, let me say that many people have asked me to explain to them how they can tell whether or not they are properly coping with intimidation. I designed the test below to help them determine for themselves the answer to this question. Perhaps you, too, might want to test yourself.

How Are You Faring With Intimidation?

1) Do you often wake up in reception rooms and find that you've been sucking your thumb and playing with a yo-yo?

2) Are you repeatedly invited to dinner, only to discover that you're the first course on the menu?

3) Do you ask your attorney's permission before going to the bathroom?

4) Are you working harder and harder, but just getting older?

5) Are you in awe of people who wear white hats?

6) Do you often ask your mirror:

   "Mirror, mirror
    On the wall,
    Who has the best positive attitude
    Of them all?"

   . . . only to have your mirror answer back: "Bullshit."

7) Do you find yourself panting excessively whenever a Court Holder enters the room?

8) Did you go to the last costume party dressed as a hare?

9) Do you walk around feeling secure because so many people have told you, "Don't worry, I'll take care of you"?

10) Are you often selected to be the patient in operations that are remembered by the slogan: "The operation was successful, but the patient died"?

11) When your house went up in flames and the firemen came crashing through to save you, were you sitting in your favorite easy chair playing the fiddle?

12) When you get hungry, do you resort to chasing squirrels?

13) Do you find yourself bluffing more but walking away with less?

14) When you were a little boy, did you always want to grow up to be a good ol' boy?

15) Do you bark a lot at closings?

What's the grading scale? Well, if you answered either "yes" *or* "no" to any of the above fifteen questions, you flunked. It was just a trick test to see, at the very least, if I got the Ice Ball Theory across to you. No matter what your feeling is about the rest of my philosophy, you salvaged something from this book if you can just face the reality that nothing you do is going to matter 50 billion years from now, anyway. Relax. Cool it. Don't take yourself so seriously . . . it's just a game.

Oops! Gotta be running along now . . . just saw an opening to the left of some hare; have to keep moving while he's still daydreaming.

Maybe I'll be seeing you around the jungle from time to time and we might even have a go at a game of intimidation together. If you aren't able to recognize me by my black-rimmed sunglasses, black suit and black briefcase, you can always spot me by the frog tattoo on my shell.